GOD AT WORK

Philip Cody SM

GOD AT WORK

Christian Marriage and Family for Partners and Parents

ST PAULS

*If you wish to respond to material in this book, or share your ideas/
stories/helpful practices as partners or parents, you may like to write to:*
Fr Phil Cody SM, c/- Cerdon, 78 Hobson St, Wellington,
Aotearoa/New Zealand

GOD AT WORK
Christian Marriage and Family for Partners and Parents
© Philip Cody SM, 1993

First published, January 1994

Scripture texts are taken from the *New Jerusalem Bible*, published and copyright
© 1985 by Darton, Longman and Todd Ltd and Doubleday & Co Inc, and are
used by permission of the publishers. Excerpts from *The Jerusalem Bible*, copyright © 1966 by Darton, Longman & Todd, Ltd and Doubleday, a division of
Bantam Doubleday Dell Publishing Group, Inc. Reprinted by permission.

National Library of Australia
Cataloguing-in-Publication Data:
Cody, Philip, 1944-
God at Work: Christian Marriage and family for partners and parents
ISBN 1 875570 25 X
1. Marriage — Religious aspects — Christianity. 2. Family — Religious life.
I. Title.
248.4

Cover photo: Del Canale, © Periodici San Paolo, Milan, Italy
Cover design: Bruno Colombari SSP

Published by
ST PAULS — Society of St Paul,
60-70 Broughton Road — (PO Box 230) — Homebush, NSW 2140

ST PAULS is an activity of the Priests and Brothers of the Society of St Paul
who proclaim the Gospel through the media of social communication.

I dedicate this book to all
Christian Couples and their Families
with the prayer that they may
grow in Love and Life.
I write it with thanks
to my parents,
to my brother and sister
and their families,
and to the many married couples and their children
who help me experience
the Church as Family.

I thank particularly
John and Penny, Terry and Mary, Adrian and Catherine
who helped in the final writing.

In thanking God
for letting me write it,
I place
'God at Work: Christian Marriage and Family
for Partners and Parents'
under the Patronage of
Joachim and Anne,
grandparents of Jesus.

CONTENTS

INTRODUCTION

This text has been fifteen years in developing. Over that time it has been changed and added to. Everyone was willing to talk about marriage with me and had something to say! Married school friends, doctors and their partners, people in parishes and on holiday, people in England, Ireland, Italy, Aotearoa/New Zealand and Australia, people met in a Liverpool night shelter and the London Underground, Christian groups like Neo-Catechumenate, Focolare Movement, Marriage Encounter, other Christian ministers and their partners, my own married relations and their families, couples of a Christian Marriage Program and, most recently, couples of Emmanuel Covenant Community in Brisbane.

This book celebrates a journey. The journey of my life. I have never been too far from the reality of marriage and family life. As someone pointed out to me: 'Look at your photo albums! One family after another! You haven't just sat back and theorised about marriage. You've been in, boots an' all – visiting, staying with, bringing in the washing, taking your days off with families!'

It's true! I'm naturally a 'people person'. I love a party or family gathering.

That natural bent goes deeper into a heartfelt conviction of the important place of marriage and family life today. The Religious Family I belong to, the Society of Mary, or Marists as we are popularly known, has committed itself to work alongside the laity, the down-to-earth men and women of the Church. That has naturally suited me. I feel strongly that a priest lacks the opportunity to be warmly human without contact with family life and some close sharing with married men and women and having the opportunity to relate to children. That is what gives me life — life I hope you find echoed throughout this book. All of the examples come from personal experiences. They are a window to reflect on the spiritual theology of marriage.

So when I had the chance to work for a doctorate in January of the New Zealand summer, 1978, I naturally asked a married couple what they thought would be valuable to study for the good of married people and the Church. 'Well,' they said, 'if you could explain something of how God works in Christian marriage, that would be valuable.'

Hence the title of this book, *God at Work*. I now invite you to join me as we explore that subject. In that way a study that began with married people will come back to them again.

'Hold it, I'm not convinced! What's a priest doing, writing on marriage?', you still might wonder. As a couple queried one day after Eucharist, 'You can't have the practical experience necessary to write about marriage. What does a priest know about it?' To be honest, he knows nothing about it from the inside. I have shared in a little of marriage, but by no means all!

Therefore, the idea struck me. Let me write the book with the constant help of married people. Not only has what is written come from married partners' lives, but the final drafting has taken place over three months, working alongside three couples. I see myself as an editor, presenting on the one hand the theology of marriage, and on the other, relaying the real life situations of married people who have shared something of their lives with me.

I hope the result will encourage you to live your own marriage more fully. You can reflect on the theology, make it your own and develop it. At the end of each section there are questions to talk about with your partner. These could be used in a study group or with other couples. They are designed to help you renew your love by sharing as a couple. The questions are written by married people, so come out of the experience of marriage. The questions are of different types so some will suit you. You may be moved to make some changes in your attitude and behaviour for your own sake and the sake of your family.

Goal

The goal of this book is to affirm and encourage Christian married couples. I hope it will help married people be more convinced of the value of their lives. If you are enabled to let God work more fully in your life, the book will have been a success. *God at Work* is not an instruction manual of what to **do** to make marriage, or God for that matter, work! It is rather an **invitation to let God work** in your marriage and family.

Married couples are the ones living the theology of marriage. The first part of each section gives experiences which couples can identify with or parallel from their own lives. This will help them realise they are the real theologians of Christian Marriage. They can then deepen their own spirituality and reflection on their marriage. So, this book combines lived experience with spiritual reflection. It provides the human basis for spiritual growth as married persons and for becoming better partners.

One of the first persons I spoke with said that what couples expected of their marriage was vital. I hope this book will help couples gain a stronger positive expectation of their marriage; that it works and works well. Some reading this book will be able to celebrate what has happened in their marriage. Others may feel a bit disappointed or even despair at whether their situation will ever measure up. Be gentle on yourselves! I pray this book is a challenge which will encourage you to take another step onwards, or to open your hearts to let God work there.

Somewhere there will be a starting point. I am intending to touch those partners who are trying to succeed, sometimes failing, sometimes sinning, sometimes feeling very far from the perfect Christian couple. The ones daily taking up the love of yesterday and trying to make that love grow.

I believe many ordinary couples need assurance that it is a good thing to be permanently married and faithful to each other despite struggles with relationships, with themselves and their teenagers, and being faced with economic and employment difficulties. Assurance that they can still have children and grow in love and forgiveness and build up family life.

It is to such couples that my book is dedicated, 'so that they may grow in love'. God will bring about this growth in love by working in their marriages.

Christian couples

This book is aimed at committed Christian couples. One of the unique things about the contents is that it is Christian. Much has been written about marriage that is very helpful and practical, but *God at Work* is directed at giving a special Christian flavour to being married.

You are therefore urged to pray as you read. There is a bookmark which can be used as a prayer before you start to read, or prayed whenever seems right for you. It reminds us that God **is** at work in Christian Marriage, even as we read, no matter the various reactions I may be having to what I read. It is a prayer to invite God to work to enlighten you by what you are reading, or to show you what needs to be done in your marriage and family.

I have taken a Catholic basis. I trust other Christians will not let that distract them from finding much that will help them. Some of the references use Catholic terms. My main theological source is a text of the Second Vatican Council.[1] Although this Vatican Council was nearly thirty years ago, many of us have not yet fully appreciated its richness in our lives. *God at Work* concentrates on one source for enrichment, a special section on marriage and family in *The Constitution on the Church in the Modern World*. We use numbers 47 to 52. It is quoted throughout the book, for example (47,1), which means number 47, paragraph 1.

I am not writing directly for single parents, separated or divorced persons. I hope to strengthen Christian couples

---

1   The Constitution on the Church in the Modern World, (Gaudium et Spes), from *Vatican Council II. The Conciliar and Post-Conciliar Documents*, Austin Flannery, OP, Gen ed, Costello, Dublin, 1975.

who will be the ones to assist one-parent families, contact the divorced and care for their children, as well as be strong enough to help married partners in serious difficulty. At the same time, because the whole point of the book is to let God work in marriage and family, whenever a Christian partner is committed to God, God will work.

Outline

Each chapter, or section, contains three main parts. First, **EXPERIENCE**, some stories and cases from married people's lives. Then, **SPIRITUAL REFLECTION**, some deeper spiritual and theological considerations. Lastly, **ACTION**, with questions for shared discussion and putting into practice what you have read.

The themes of **love** and **community** unify this book. The opening chapter outlines the love of husband and wife and how God is at work there. Then a chapter on God at work in the community of the family. The last chapter reflects on God at work through Love and Community, in Jesus, the Spirit, the Church and in our mission beyond the family.

Happy reading and reflection!

1

GOD AT WORK THROUGH THE LOVE OF HUSBAND AND WIFE

1. The graciousness of God
2. The love of husband and wife
3. The personal affection of husband and wife
4. The unity and fidelity of husband and wife
5. The sexuality of husband and wife
6. The daily life of couples

1. THE GRACIOUSNESS OF GOD

- EXPERIENCE

The practical graciousness of God

There is nothing like what I call a 'crunch time' to test character! When the going gets tough and relationships are stretched. The same applies to marriage. The test of God's working is the crunch time. Talk about love is all very well. Is God there when it is uphill going? In fact, God is usually present in a very practical way.

This became clear to me listening to Fina and Paul. Paul has bone cancer and struggles with tiredness and the pain of arthritis as well. Fina and Paul have five beautiful children aged from four to sixteen. They are living proof of the practical graciousness of God at work in a marriage.

'The mental strain of wondering if Paul will be here next year, or even next month, is terrible,' Fina shared, as we sat at table together. 'The difficulty of what to say to the kiddies who wonder why "Daddy isn't getting better". The hopeless feeling of seeing someone you love in pain!' Both of them had tears in their eyes. We faced raw truth. No fancy frills to faith in God's love for them here!

Their belief in the presence of God was evident. It helps them survive, make brave decisions about treatment, carry on as normal a married and family life as possible. The 'practical graciousness of God'? Well, Fina gave evidence of the support they were receiving: knowing people care about them; the nurse who regularly comes for injections; the Church family; people asking how Paul is and how Fina herself is coping; the baking that arrives; looking after the children. As so often happens, God is at work through the love and practical care of other people.

Daily loving

The Love or gracious presence of God is shown in daily loving. I do not know about you, but I need to learn that again and again. It is in the routine things that I struggle with each day, that I need to discover God's Love. As Julie, mother of five said, 'There's an enormous difference between the romantic courting days and the often shattering reality of sharing every minute of every day with your partner. Trying to be more loving is what life is all about. As your love grows each day, you find you really want to live your life around your partner. The daily giving of yourself is the most successful way we know'.

That daily expression of God's Love can take various forms: giving strength to cope, making a couple able to work through arguments that come up, drawing the couple closer, giving stability at home and in business, providing moral support in all things, deciding what direction to take for the family, accepting God's ways when hardships hit.

That practical, gracious love is nurtured by prayer. Ellen and her husband, Eric, told me how they had learnt during their married life to read Scripture and look for guidance from it. They shared their prayer and spiritual experiences. That daily love laid the foundation for now because, with her husband dead, Ellen is rewarded with a sense of union with Eric. As she confirmed, 'Eric has completed the spiritual journal. He has made it into the real play and not, like us, still rehearsing'! Wow! Give me that sort of faith! Help me in my daily rehearsing!!

One of the easily remembered guidelines for a growing marriage, presented by a couple on a preparation for marriage course, was: P-rayer, P-illow talk and P-artnership. The three 'P's! P-artnership sets the theme. P-illow talk is a reminder to ensure some loving communication took place at the end of the day, and P-rayer.

It is not necessary to kneel down or be very formal when praying. Some pray on the way to work; some while doing the housework. As long as partners pray together at some time. One couple suggested the ideal time was lying in bed at the end of the day. I thought this a pretty good idea until I mentioned it to one couple. The husband said, 'That's all very nice, but as soon as I lie down, I fall straight asleep!'

• SPIRITUAL REFLECTION

The graciousness of God

Marriage confers grace. Grace means gift. God's loving presence is a gift to us. Grace is really the gracious life of God within us. The love of husband and wife shares in that gracious Love of God. In marriage, husband and wife become renewed, gifted, graced persons. They live by God's life! God is at work in them as people who know the graciousness, the kindness, of God's presence with them.

> The Lord, wishing to bestow special gifts of grace and divine love on [married love] has restored, perfected and elevated it (49,1).

To say husband and wife are graced persons means that they love with the Love of God. As graced persons, they share in the presence of the personal Love of Jesus Christ. The Spirit works in them through Love to transform them and their whole lives. This gracious, loving presence is felt in good times and bad.

The partner's love for each other is now directed to God. Partners discover and receive God's Love in their love. For a couple graced in this way the words of John's First Letter are strikingly true:

> My dear friends, let us love one another
> since love is from God
> and everyone who loves
> is a child of God and knows God. . .
> As long as we love one another
> God remains in us
> and God's love comes to its perfection in us
> (1 Jn 4:7, 12).

This is what is meant by Jesus healing and perfecting the love of spouses by grace or the life of Love. They are rendered capable of true loving. As graced persons, their love is now gracious, married love which is to be exercised in the whole of their life.

Once Jesus Christ's Love is present in partners, their whole life is changed. Their daily life becomes more loving and less selfish. Couples find the 'outstanding courage . . . required for the constant fulfilment of the duties of this Christian calling' (49,2). Marriage has its difficulties and its participants need help. 'Spouses, therefore, will need grace for leading a holy life' (49,2).

In other words, there is provided the proper means to fulfil Christian married life. This gift of God's Love continually renders a spouse fit to be a good husband or wife, father or mother. It is designed to make their daily love 'firm, generous, prompt to sacrifice' (49,2).

The gracious Love of God touches those demanding areas of marriage, the tiredness that drains strength and charity, the wear and tear and dulling effect of habit, of knowing what the other partner will say, how s/he will act. It brings a freshness and ability to forgive each other's failings and prevents small vendettas leading to strife. Gracious Love helps wife and husband rise above these so they can live a full Christian life. Grace brings the humility to say 'Sorry' or 'I forgive you, let's begin again'. As graced persons, the partners repeat Jesus' own action with one another. That is, they restore love, they perfect each other and so their love is strengthened. Without Jesus Christ's actual loving presence it is hard to make marriage succeed; with it, the couple is more capable of succeeding and growing in love.

It is vital to note that this access to grace is the ordinary plan for Christian couples. Christian marriage has this natural claim on God's Love permanently attached to it. The couple has the exact grace needed to complete their lives. We could apply to Christian partners the statement Paul says God spoke to him: 'My grace is enough for you...' (2 Cor 12:9). God has graced husband and wife with the Love of Jesus Christ as the ordinary way to help them live Christian married life to the full.

Christian spouses, you have a special vocation containing the pledge of God's support. God is not ignorant of the various difficulties and obstacles of relationship, economics and bringing up a family. God provides in the Love of Jesus the precise help you need.

Living and praying

To be really graced people, Christian partners should do two things: live out their married life and pray for that gift of Jesus' Love.

They will eagerly practise a love that is firm, generous
and prompt to sacrifice and will ask for it in their prayers
(49,2).

It is by practice that we grow in love. Married love is
developed and increased by exercising it. Couples are to pray
for Jesus Christ to come and help them, to grace them by
his continued presence in their lives. This is putting into
practice the Lord's counsel 'Ask and it will be given to you'
(Mt 7:7). It brings results, as many will testify.

It is important for couples to know how to pray. As a
guideline, I would suggest that husband and wife pray at
least one Our Father together each day. Over and above
that, they may feel free to share a prayer in their own words
for each other, for a sick child, for others in need. The Our
Father is a beautiful prayer and one that partners of different
Christian denominations can pray togther.

Especially when the children come along, it is vital for
them to see Mum or Dad joining in a prayer. This guideline
stems from Jesus' own teaching on how to pray (Lk 11:1-4).
There is something special about being in the presence of
Jesus in each other and being able to pray in your own
words. Many do not pray this way. How to do it? By
starting!

We have the guidance of the book of Tobit (8:5-7) where
Tobias exhorted his wife, Sarah, to get up and pray with
him to God for grace and protection. Whenever a spouse
has a problem, he or she can always say a quiet prayer to
God. Each has a privileged place before God. Each has a
special power to represent the needs of the other. I wonder
how many couples have fully tapped this power. Have you?

ACTION

(i) The term 'gracious' is not used much these days.
What images does that word bring to mind?
Relate some ways in which God has shown gracious-
ness to me individually or to us as a couple.
How am I gracious in my relationship with my spouse?

(ii) Some people become dejected when they read 'They
will eagerly practise a love that is firm, generous and
prompt to sacrifice' (49,2).
They become dejected because they see how far they
fall short of this ideal.
They become so dejected that they forget the part that
says '[They] will ask for it in their prayers'.
Do we ask for it in our prayers?
How could we ask more often or more faithfully?

(iii) How could we, as a couple, change things so that we
experience more of 'this help of Jesus Christ's actual
loving presence'?

2. THE LOVE OF HUSBAND AND WIFE

• EXPERIENCE

The prime task of a couple is to love each other

This heading may seem rather obvious. Well, I thought so too, until a friend who had been involved with counselling, personal formation work and Marriage Encounter for over twenty years, gave his opinion of the key task for a married couple: 'If they really want to deepen their Christian Marriage, be best able to help their children and build up their family, their prime task is to love each other, even before God!'

This stopped me in my tracks! I had usually heard it the other way round: first God and then the spouse. He was insistent! As he explained, Christian Marriage is so designed that the couple discovers God **in** each other. His point is perhaps seen more clearly where a partner is intensely caught up in Church, school and pastoral affairs, all for the love of God, but his or her partner and children do not get much of their time.

Another man on retreat realised he had his priorities wrong when he drew a picture of himself up a mountain in contact with God. His adviser showed him he had his back to his wife and family who were still down below! Love of God without love of neighbour is incomplete love. 'Whoever does not love the brother/sister whom they can see, cannot love God, whom they have not seen . . . whoever loves God, must also love their brother/sister' (1 Jn 4:20f). Of course, the emphasis can be just as wrong the other way around. It is false love to choose someone over against God.

So, while the Christian husband and wife will have a personal relationship to God and his/her own prayer life, the challenge of marriage will be to receive what God is doing in their life through their partner. In turn, a partner's key duty is to grow in love of God by the gift of themselves to their spouse.

Accepting a 'Third Person' who sets couples free

'I really think this is what makes Christian Marriage different,' said Ted, 'two people accepting God as a "Third Person" in their marriage. When Jesus comes, he brings life and a source of power for each of us.'

The Person of Jesus can help us work through the real difficulties of marriage, difficulties such as Isabel outlined: 'I get so miserable at times, I just don't know what to do,' she said through tears. 'I know they're small things but they all add up. It's a real struggle. Andrew and I both have to work and sometimes his shift means he can't be home to see the children much. I worry about the children's future and whether I'm doing the right things for them. Suddenly the builder sent in a bill for double what we thought it would cost. I feel like going away by myself'.

This sort of situation makes it vital for couples like Isabel and Andrew to be very conscious of the help of Jesus for each other, binding them closer even when, at this stage, they cannot be together as much as they would like.

A striking example of the effect of true love of husband and wife was the marriage of Tim and Mary. Mary had cancer and was dying. They reflected on the meaning of life and shared many sad and joyous times. Once Tim plucked up the courage to say as he sat on the side of the bed, 'You know, Mary, when you have died, I think I will become a priest'. This brought forth a rippling chuckle from Mary. Tim was rather put out after his serious comment and stopped short. Mary explained. 'No! Stick with what you are good at. Get married again!' What a freeing tribute to his love for her. 'Stick with what you are good at.' Tim is, in fact, happily re-married.

• **SPIRITUAL REFLECTION**

God at work through love and life

A most important point for Christian couples is that God is at work through their love for each other. God works in a human way, whether it be through their affection or prayer, their sexuality or role as parents. Christian couples are to recognise God transforming these areas from within their marriage.

Everything we have said about marriage and the family can be summed up in two words: **love** and **life**.

God works through the love of the spouses to set up with them a community of love and life. As well as helping them set up that community, God continues to work with them in it. Here we see the link of the themes of love and community.

If you like, marriage may be symbolised by the marriage rings interlocked to form a community of love and life.

COMMUNITY OF

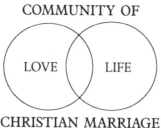

CHRISTIAN MARRIAGE

The married state is 'the intimate partnership of life and love (which) has been established by the Creator' (48,1). In other words, God works through the love of the spouses because God designed their life and love. Right away we see an intimate connection of love and life. True community involves intimacy. In Christian Marriage we have a divinely planned community of life and love.

Love in God's plan is naturally ordered to life. God works with the couple to bring about a unity which is fruitful. God cooperates with the partners in love to produce life.

> By its very nature ... married love is ordered to the procreation and education of offspring and it is in them that it finds its crowning glory (48,1).

> (Without intending to underestimate the other ends of marriage), true married love ... is directed to disposing the spouses to co-operate valiantly with the love of the Creator ... who through them will increase and enrich his family (50,1).

It is evident there is a link of love and life, especially in children.

Perhaps a practical way the church can recognise and value this intimacy of love and life is by priests and ministers blessing the baby in the mother's womb. Pregnancy is an important time and God's Love must be seen to be present in a practical way. Church interest in the baby should not start at birth. There needs to be some Christian sharing in all the practical, medical, clothing, dietary preparation that takes place.

Today we are becoming very aware of being the church. This will deepen our desire to help each other. Perhaps a Christian Mothers' Group within a parish can take particular note of those mothers who are pregnant. They might offer them help. Each situation will have its own needs.

One example that is especially helpful is giving the parents a little time to themselves. Someone can take care of any children they already have, even for a short while any one day, or during hospital visits.

A prayer for, and blessing of, the mother and the baby are part of that. The father's presence is key. He himself has a magnificent opportunity to be an instrument of God's Love by frequently supporting his wife and blessing and talking to his unborn child in her womb. God works harmoniously with the love of the partners. Clear statements about the value of children are a safeguard in an age which seems to play down the importance of children.

> Christians today are overjoyed, and so too are all who esteem conjugal and family life highly, to witness the various ways in which progress is being made in fostering those partnerships of love and in encouraging reverence for human life (47,1).

From the start, the marriage community is seen as one valuing love and life. You cannot truly love without openness to life, nor have a happy life without love.

The witness of God's Love
to husband and wife and others

God is at work through the community of love and life of the couple to witness God's presence to them and to all whom they meet.

> Marriage is not merely for the procreation of children; its nature as an indissoluble compact between the people and the good of the children demands that the mutual love of the partners be properly shown, that it should grow and mature (50,3).

God will ensure this balance within Christian Marriage. God will assist married partners to show that proper order of life and love to each other. How important for Christian couples to be aware of this and to invite God to work fully in their life and love.

Jesus can enter difficult situations and manifest God's Love and support to the couple. 'Come to me, all you who labour and are overburdened, and I will give you rest' (Mt 11:28).

God is also at work with the couple to reveal God to others:

> [The Christian family] will show forth to all Christ's living presence in the world . . . by the love and generous fruitfulness of the spouses (48,4).

> Authentic married love will be held in high esteem . . . if Christian spouses give outstanding witness to faithfulness and harmony in their love, if they are conspicuous in their concern for the education of their children (49,3).

> Thus in the footsteps of Christ, the principle of life, (married people) will bear witness by their faithful love

> . . . to that mystery of love which the Lord revealed to the
> world by his death and resurrection (52,7).

All these quotations link the themes of love and life. They
make clear that Christian Marriage must witness to love.

While it is important to see the human way God helps
spouses set up a community of love and life, we must beware
of bringing God's activity down to a purely human level.
Although God aids the couple to develop a fully human
community, God reminds them that marriage has a trans-
cendent note about it. That is, it will be a marriage that
has an eternal vision and goal.

> Let all be convinced that human life and its transmission
> are realities whose meaning is not limited by the horizons
> of this life only; their true evaluation and full meaning
> can only be understood in reference to our eternal destiny
> (51,4).

Here is a vital principle. The fully human involves eternal
vision: the eternal is present in the fully human.

However, partners should not have unreal expectations
of each other or of marriage itself. Despite the popular
saying, a partner cannot give the other 'heaven on earth'.
With a vision that sees full happiness only in heaven, the
couple will not be disappointed by the inadequacies they
discover in each other and in marriage and family life. An
eternal vision frees partners to appreciate their humanness.

This is not something that only those with great faith
will realise or recognise. Faith is necessary to live it whole-
heartedly; only then can we see God working with us. What
will be produced by those with an eternal outlook will be
a delightfully human marriage, recognised by non-believers.

ACTION

(i) 'God works through the love of the spouses to set up with them a community of love.'
If I believed this more fully, how would my behaviour change?
Is there any change I would be willing to make now in order to act out this belief?

(ii) A married couple said: 'I don't think we've ever stopped worrying about caring for our children long enough to think about the eternal significance of it all. Maybe we're missing the real meaning of what we've been about.'
Could we be missing the full and true meaning of our life together too?

(iii) Are there ways in which we can show strongly, both in our own family and to others, the intimate connection between love and life?

3. THE PERSONAL AFFECTION OF HUSBAND AND WIFE

- EXPERIENCE

Just for today, Jesus

We need to have a sense of dignity of each person we meet. I learnt some home truths about that when I missed a train in Liverpool and ended up in the night shelter under the city's huge cathedral. It was an invaluable experience to be on the receiving end and getting the soup dished out to me!

Night shelters can be depressing places. Here I discovered rough humanity often surfaces and a sense of dignity can go out the window. My idea of the poor being united and caring for one another was rudely shattered. The end of a cigarette can start a fight or a torrent of abuse.

Yet here there can be fun, warmth and wisdom. Dignity in human relationship could be found. I saw that in Old Jim. Once a sailor, Jim would tell tales of distant lands if you wanted to listen. He could calmly roll a cigarette as though he owned the world and not just the sack bag at the end of the mattress.

'Jim, what's the solution to the problems of the people here?' 'Well, it's like the song,' he pondered, 'just for today, Jesus, just for today.' I think that often applies to marriage and family life, too. Dignity and love find expression in human affection just for today.

'You know,' one older married partner commented to me, 'I think it's the loving goodness between the spouses that makes marriage. We need to respect each other and be kind to each other. This overflows to our children.' Any undermining of the personal value of one parent in front of the children is bad. A comment such as, 'Sean doesn't really know how to handle children', said before a child who really needs to admire his father, can do damage.

'Respect for each other helps us acknowledge our differences,' said Tony to me. 'Men often think affection is just a physical thing, so at the first touch we are already thinking of bed and sex. In fact Jean is simply beginning a process of intimate sharing. She tells me clearly if I don't listen to her first. Otherwise, all the chocolates and flowers in the world aren't worth a thing! I'm slowly seeing what's important for her is our relationship and the value of honesty I show her as a person equal to me. Jean once shared with me how her father used to tap her under the chin when she would express her point of view, thinking he was being very affectionate. In fact she felt belittled and found it destructive. He wasn't recognising her as a person with worth. The last thing I want to do is carry on like that. I've had to learn showing affection means recognising dignity too. We need each other. Jean needs my physical presence. I need her intimate sharing.'

The kitchen sink

Affection can take place in very ordinary daily events. There is quite enough in each day to test the couple's ability to communicate with love, respect and support. For example, some of the most precious family moments may take place in the kitchen or around the kitchen sink. Mind you, the kitchen can also be a very stressful time and place. It is often enough to cope with the demands of getting people fed, let alone the tension of putting the children to bed. Nevertheless, the kitchen is a central point for communication. Often this centres on the dishes. Even with a dish-washing machine, it is still possible to learn how to share and contribute. Doing dishes is important. Some married couples find the kitchen is the place they can talk and share at the end of the working day.

Many have an array of plants and odds and ends on the bench or shelf near the kitchen sink. This will often include a holy picture or a little prayer. Part of the one my mother had is:

> Lord of all pots and pans and things,
>   Since I've not time to be
> A Saint by doing lovely things
>   Or watching late with thee. . .
> Make me a saint by getting meals
>   And washing up the plates. . .
> Warm all the kitchen with thy Love,
>   And light it with thy peace.
> Forgive me all my worrying
>   And make my grumbling cease.
> Thou who didst love to give us food
>   In room or by the sea,
> Accept this service that I do;
>   I do it unto Thee.

Another special time where affection means a lot, is in pregnancy. It is warm and tender to see a husband sensitively supporting his wife at this time. As I overhead one man in a hospital waiting room say, with one hand on his wife's tummy, 'How's she moving?'

This is how some couples see affection 'permeating their whole lives' (49,1): God works through their partner's 'gentleness and understanding', through 'companionship', 'sharing', 'intimacy', 'comforting each other', 'consideration', 'caring and looking after each other'.

Showing affection is a real choice to love your partner. It requires practice. Couples have their happiness at stake. They are to be single-minded about loving each other with affection. This commitment might be to a formal time for communicating feelings and the good things of their lives, as well as for facing difficult areas. Couples may need to get help and counselling for this. A lot of times, there will be informal expressions of affection: time together on the couch, a choice to love each other by positive, affectionate words to each other or a hug. Affection needs to be expressed or love will die!

Growing in sharing affection

'When we first fell in love,' recalled Pat, 'Tim and I couldn't get close enough. We would walk hand in hand or just let our shoulders touch. It was such a joy when we snuggled our shoulders together.

Then slowly we distanced after marriage. The joke about the way married people sit apart in the car was true. We would shy away from affectionate touches.

What changed for us? At first we delighted in each other. It was easy to respect the dignity of each other and even easier to show that affectionately. Then the normal pressures of marriage and relationship caught us up. Our first attraction wore thin. Unconscious obstacles to showing affection reared their head, such as lack of receiving affection when we were little. Signs that at first seemed so loving, became empty and even annoying, and so we drew apart. It was only when we faced the truth about ourselves, learnt to show that honestly and with trust, that we rediscovered our affection. We arrived at a deeper affection than the constant physical closeness of our first love. Our faith in God and asking God's help not only strengthened the healing of our self-image, but made us see true value in each other. Now, thanks be to God, we're not afraid to show affection. We know how each other feels about things. We find peace by praying together, holding hands. We are sure God's there.'

• SPIRITUAL REFLECTION

Affection recognises human dignity

God works through the spouses' personal affection. Affection is a visible sign of true love for someone. Affection expresses respect and value for them as a person who has dignity. Affection is not just a physical thing. Nor is it simply a sign like flowers or chocolates. It may be expressed in those ways, but primarily it is an external expression of a prior, inner relationship, a relationship which builds on recognising the personal dignity of someone.

> The unity of marriage ... is made clear in the equal personal dignity which must be accorded to man and wife in mutual and unreserved affection (49,2).

It is through affection that personal dignity is recognised and expressed. God can reaffirm a person's dignity and self-worth through all that partners say to each other and how they show their respect and love for one another. God is the one who permeates the couple's affection with Love:

> A love like that, [that is, restored by God], bringing together the human and divine, leads the partners to a free and mutual giving of self experienced in tenderness and action, and permeates their whole lives' (49,1).

Christian partners are encouraged to show this selfless affection because 'this love is actually developed and increased by the exercise of it' (49,1).

> [The nature of marriage] as an indissoluble compact between two people and the good of the children demand that the mutual love of the partners be properly shown, that it should grow and mature (50,3).

Rather than burning itself out in a flare of passion, true affection is enduring because it is integrated into the whole person. When spouses are striving to love each other and their children in a fully human way, God can be said to work through their personal affection.

God has created us as persons with equal dignity (49,2). God is present and alive in each person. God works through the personality of the spouses. Loving affection embraces the whole person. God helps each partner to love the other for their value as a person.

Perhaps the great challenge of reaching the full dignity of human relationship is to let our true personality come through our psychological and physical make-up, and to reach the depth of the other person. We could set it out in the following diagram:

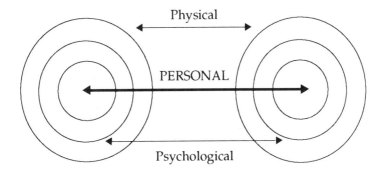

Each set of circles represents a person, you or me. We consist of physical and psychological elements (the outer circles) and a deeper, personal me (the inner circle). We can have various types of relationships with others depending on which level we relate to them. What we are aiming at is a person to person relationship. The beauty of a fully personal relationship is that it is **me** who loves and expresses myself at an affective (psychological) and physical level.

For the Christian husband or wife, the added task is to grow into the person of Jesus Christ and to allow Jesus to develop the person of their partner. For example, a hug is not only a physical squeeze. It may express security or affection. Above all, it should be me. 'I love you', and this hug means that. The more I am like Christ and open to him, the more that hug can mean 'God loves you'. God works through husband and wife to show personal Love for them.

This is the value of movements like Marriage Encounter which gives a couple the chance to rediscover and live out how each feels and how there is a real power in Jesus in their marriage.

We make a decision to show affection. This is important, because at times we certainly will not feel like it. Our choice lays the ground for setting up a habit of love. It is a bit like setting out the boxing for pouring concrete. We decide to act in an affectionate way and God will work through us to seal the love.

God ensures a couple grows in affection. God works through their personal love. That is how God is seen to be at work. I learn of God's Love through the signs of genuine affection shown me. If I am the one showing affection, I learn of God's Love in that I become conscious of God working through me.

Human signs of affection

God treats us as human beings. God's presence is shown humanly. God works through the 'eminently human love' (49,1) of the couple. The love engendered by God is truly human, not a casual act, nor fiery passion. Nor does eminent mean divine or angelic. It is down to earth human, with the sublime value that embodies.

In other words, God's working within the love of the couple does not ignore or destroy what is human. It enhances it. Spouses are meant to be human. They are meant to love each other in a fully or eminently human way. There is something divine about that.

Grasping this is essential to understanding how God works in Christian Marriage. God works in a **human** way. An example of this is childbirth. Childbirth is an enormously powerful moment with great bonding emotions for mother, father and baby. Who will deny God is at work then? Things could not get much more human for the couple than this time. Hence, God is present.

Other cases of affection have a definite spiritual aspect to them. One area where this is evident is within the Charismatic Renewal. Spouses will testify to healed relationships or other direct answers to prayers. Contact with God combines the spiritual and the human. Worship on our side; adoption on God's. There is often some physical, human sign after some more directly spiritual action. For example, after Reconciliation, or a formal seeking of God's forgiveness, there will often be an experienced peace and greater ease between partners.

God is present in us and works through all that is human: the 'Good Mornings', little signs of love, the kiss, the hug, doing the washing, caring for the sick child, discussing financial problems, meeting others who come home, the joy, the pain, the teenager leaving home, the marriage anniversary.

What a difference that makes! The way I dress, the signs of tenderness I show my partner, my concern for a clean home, the way I work, my respect of myself, the friends I have, remembering the anniversary, the interest I take in my son or daughter's homework or choice of vocation, sensitivity to show love to my partner; all is changed and becomes a vehicle of offering God's Love and accepting God's Love for me through my partner. The human becomes fully human and I find God working at the heart of marriage.

A couple should not be afraid to be human. This applies both to the acceptance of their own personalities and failings and the loving acceptance of the humanness of their partner. We can be all too easily upset by weakness, difficulties in relationships, falling out or our very ordinariness. Where God enters in, there is the ability to forgive, start again, grow in love, trying to let God work more through our own humanness and giving in love.

Christian partners can be encouraged by the growth of St Paul in recognising and accepting his weakness. Paul went beyond that state of acceptance to see that God actually used his weakness to show that God's power was working in him. 'It is, then, about my weaknesses that I am happiest of all to boast, so that the power of Christ may rest upon me. . .' (2 Cor 12:9).

This may be especially troublesome for men. To accept humanness seems at times to go against the manly image cast by some. To be able to cry, to share feelings, to surrender, to be vulnerable, not to have to perform sexually at a certain level, are very important human activities that will enhance his marriage and bring a deeper loving response from his wife.

Growth in marriage

One factor that seems important here is that the marriage relationship is a growing one. Humanly, we grow and develop in life. So in marriage, partners will change and have the opportunity to grow in love. This can follow a very human path. All can be peaceful in their relationship and then a child will get sick and gradually place a strain on the parents which will affect their own relating. Human tension and weakness is part of married life.

Husband and wife should not be surprised to feel tension, anger and frustration. Christian Marriage is one of joy and tension, of peace and upset. Tensions and upsets need to be worked through and resolved. That can lead a couple to a new level of truth in their marriage. For example, we can say 'I forgive you', or 'I'm sorry', too quickly, and leave the real hurt and situation unaddressed and unresolved. So the situation will rear its head again. Christians need to repent of wrong actions or harsh words causing upset to their partner. They then need to be willing to work at changing what they can. Their aim should be to find an outcome with which both can be at peace. That is true sorrow and the ground for lasting forgiveness. It will also ensure that any affection, like a hug to express sorrow and forgiveness, is genuine.

Sometimes the last thing either partner will feel like is forgiving or praying. It is not wrong to pray with strong

feelings. It may be impossible to come to actual forgiveness, let alone feel forgiveness, before praying. As one couple
related, 'At times like this, we pray a psalm through clenched
teeth! Spontaneous prayer would not be wise'.

So, a set prayer, even when we do not want to, may bring
results. God then has space to enter in to help each
understand the other's point of view. God can bring the
help to actually forgive. Either partner's suggestion to pray
at a time like this should be accepted with good will.

Husband and wife should understand what are signs of
true growth and ask themselves, 'Am I helping my partner
grow?' Such signs include a deepening trust in one another,
respect for the needs of each other, an ability to hear what
each is saying and regular sharing.

From a Christian point of view, partners should bring
Jesus Christ consciously into their lives and relationships.
Their own growth will deepen if each spouse helps the other
to grow closer to God.

We should try not to get angry about our moods and
humanness. We all need a good dose of self-forgiveness and
self-acceptance. That possibly comes when we realise other
couples are the same. We do not have to keep up appear-
ances. God's Love comes through the love of the spouses
in a very human way and that humanness is not to be
hidden as non Christian.

What makes a marriage Christian is that, despite this
process of sometimes painful growth, the couple goes on
together, truly loving the person who sometimes can hurt
or frustrate them. They go on seeking to live out the plan
of God for them, for their family, their neighbours, their
Church and the world.

ACTION

(i) What is your definition of affection?

In your marriage, how do you experience affection from your spouse?

Does that experience meet your personal need for affection? (That is, is your personal dignity recognised and expressed?)

(ii) As well as saying, 'I forgive you', to your partner for their faults, committed Christian Marriage requires accepting a process of openness to growth.

Where do forgiveness and growth apply in your marriage?

4. THE UNITY AND FIDELITY OF HUSBAND AND WIFE

• EXPERIENCE

Unity in marriage

When I come to think about the faithful love a husband and wife need to have in a lasting marriage and family life, I recall an incident that took place on the London Underground. I was travelling with a rucksack and had a cross on my lapel. A fairly rugged young man got on the train and he immediately said, 'Cor, a travellin' vicar'!

We started chatting and I eventually asked, 'What do you think is the means to make marriage last?' 'Two strong brothers,' he replied. 'Oh? Explain to me,' I enquired. 'Well, our sister was being belted by her husband, but me and me brother paid a visit on him. Not too Christian, mind, but it worked!'

I'm not advocating that, but I could not help admiring his concern for his sister's marriage. As he said, 'Too many folk forget their family once they're married'. Maybe if we were more supportive, there would not be the huge fallout rate in marriage today. I sometimes wonder if we are almost accepting that marriage will break up! As Christians we must not slip into a worldly attitude of 'I'll give it a go, but if it doesn't work out. . .' God did not design things that way. God has pledged help to sustain and be with us in all our needs.

That combined conviction of husband and wife to help each other remain faithful and united, covers areas like concern to give each other space to fulfil personal needs.

This requires negotiation to ensure it goes hand in hand with shared responsibility for the home and family.

I recall Andrea saying her marriage to Nicholas faced a crisis when children came along. Nicholas had slipped into a nice routine: get up; coffee; off to work; home late (after the children were in bed); eat dinner; to bed (often too preoccupied with his book to really listen to Andrea). 'We got someone in to help us in the end,' Andrea said. 'I told Nicholas we couldn't go on like this. I wanted him to be united with me in looking after the kids. Also I expected more attention than that myself.' Their experience reinforced for me that fidelity to married love involves a continuing dialogue. Couples need to keep lines of negotiation open to sustain their changing needs and responsibilities.

Togetherness

I'll never forget a trip to Scotland after work on my doctorate. It was on a boat from Oban, across to the Isle of Mull and to the famous Iona. It was a sunny day, and a delight to sit on deck in the sun and let the wind blow the tensions of solid study away. I got talking with two Japanese children who popped up with questions and then disappeared below. I discovered later they were checking in with their parents and repeating what I said! It must have been all right, because I got invited to tea and learnt some good things about togetherness as a couple.

'We believe the children [Dennis, 7, and Miriam, 4] should be in bed reasonably early,' John explained. 'They need the sleep and quite frankly it's the only chance Miyoko and I get to have time together.' Perhaps that time was all the more important because of John and Miyoko's cultural difference. They certainly were a lovely couple who had enriched each other and Dennis and Miriam. How many children do you know who speak both Japanese and English fluently? Their family was open and welcoming, as I experienced. I think that flowed from John and Miyoko's togetherness.

One way married togetherness is undermined, is by partners attacking or blaming the other. Couples can slip into comments to outsiders like, 'He's lazy'; 'She's always at her mother's!' These may be true and need to be discussed and faced together. Christian partners should be emptying themselves, to love one another and work through issues together. 'Easily said,' you might comment. True, and if it is said in love, it will clear the air. The results have lasting consequences.

As I was typing this material about togetherness and how married couples are united, I reflected it seemed a bit theoretical and hard on those spouses whose spouse had died. Just then I received a letter from Kay, a widow who expressed precisely that permanence of united togetherness:

> Terry [her deceased husband] has been very close and very much involved in everything. I now realise that marriage outlasts death. Here we are still walking the same path, aiming for the same ends. But we are on different sides of the veil that separates those who have seen God and the rest of us.

This was close to her husband's death, but I have since met others who recount similar belief. Theologically, the marriage as such has ended, but the persons who vowed to love each other still exist and exist as persons who made that relationship.

• SPIRITUAL REFLECTION

Unity and fidelity

God is at work to help couples be united and faithful. God is revealed through their unity and fidelity. We are talking about the qualities of marriage. Marriage is one (unity) and permanent (fidelity) – (an older term was indissoluble).

> The Christian family ... will show forth to all people Christ's living presence ... by the love and generous fruitfulness of the spouses [and] by their unity and fidelity (48,4).

Unity and permanence are based on the value of the person. God helps partners deeply respect each other as persons.

> The unity of marriage, distinctly recognised by the Lord, is made clear in the equal personal dignity which must be accorded to man and wife in mutual and unreserved affection (49,2).

This personal value, which lies at the basis of unity in marriage, needs special nurturing today. Society is not structured for marital unity and harmony. Enormous pressures are put on people to perform at work. This leaves a parent semi-exhausted and with limited time for spouse and children at home. Business may isolate a wife from a husband or create tensions through the high expectations placed on her. An interesting future awaits us as computer science makes it possible for more work to be done at home.

To grow as a couple, husband and wife need to grow in wholeness as a man and woman. There can be all sorts of needs in us that demand attention. Dealing with them is a life-time process. However, if those basic personal needs are not dealt with, a stressed partner will not be able to help their partner either. One example is the isolation a mother with several children can feel. Sure, she may have all sorts of mechanical aids, and the telephone and television. If she is committed to care for the home and her children, she cannot just pop out and visit someone or take time out for herself. A phone conversation can help, television may distract, but this sense of isolation cuts deeply into a woman's heart, even though the externals of the home seem to be fulfilled.

Part of that isolation is the result of choice, a choice to marry and be a mother. That demands sacrifice. Not that she minds making the sacrifice; she is happy to make it, especially if she sees and experiences the love of her husband for her and the children. A woman needs to have that sacrifice acknowledged and understood. Part of that sacrifice may possibly be not having completed higher educational studies. With society's, and even the Church's, expectations for higher education and degrees for both men and women, we might unconsciously be making it difficult for couples to nourish the basic unity and fidelity of their marriage.

Husband and wife can deal with this situation and work for personal and marriage unity by taking conscious action to value each other. They need to value each other as persons, not just for the work they do. The greeting at night needs to go deeper than 'How was the day?', to, 'How are you?' A wife at home needs to know **she** is important. What she has done is also important, especially the value of child care she provides for the family. Each of their worlds is important. Let them build a unity in listening to and valuing each other. Truly valued spouses will be able to build unity. Practical steps could be taken, for instance, for the wife to ensure she gets adult conversation. She is really helped if she can have the support of other women and mothers living nearby. That is why some Christian families cluster their homes, to share similar values and faith.

Here is a key opportunity to let God work. God can heal that deep-down isolation of a woman and mother at home, even while she is doing things like being at the clothes line. God can bring wholeness to husband and wife. God can help when it seems beyond normal capacity to cope. Husband and wife need frequently to turn to God in prayer to ask for unity.

Another way of seeing the presence of God integrating married persons is in appreciating the nature of love.

> Endorsed by mutual fidelity [married] love abides faithfully in mind and body in prosperity and adversity and hence excludes both adultery and divorce (49,2).

We will recognise the marriage promise 'for better or worse'. It is the very demands of love that render Christian Marriage one and permanent. The gift of one person to another is something definite. It has been made without reserve in its integrity; it must be without reserve in time, too.

The Church's concern for proclaiming marriage as one and permanent is to help couples attain the fullness of personal love. Married love is undertaken for 'better or worse' ('in prosperity and adversity'). This is not easy, and that is why God is at work in the couple's love. Now we can truly appreciate the weight of the words:

> [Christ abides with them] in order that by their mutual self-giving spouses will love each other with enduring fidelity (48,2).

A couple must be faithful in mind and body. One can be physically present to a spouse, but with mind and heart far away. A partner reveals his/her thinking in love to their partner. 'The married couple must practise an affectionate sharing of thought and common deliberation' (52,1). Before making a decision husband and wife should take mutual counsel. Thinking about it together comes before united action. God does not ignore normal human processes like this.

Togetherness

What we are stressing is togetherness. 'Together they render glory to God' (48,2). The Latin is *'communiter'*, calling to mind how God sets up a community of life and love. The depth of meaning in Christian Marriage is that partners cling to God together.

> Thus the man and woman, who 'are no longer two but one flesh' (Mt 19:6), help serve each other by their marriage partnership (48,1).

What Jesus Christ brings about in a couple is an intimacy of persons who will work together, think together, serve each other and thus be united and faithful to each other. In other words, togetherness.

Partners need to do things together, practise becoming better at communicating, at intimacy. If any partner reading this has slipped into the habit of newspaper or magazine reading or TV absorption, to all intent quite ignoring his or her spouse, please stop and think. 'What should I be doing to truly love my partner?' It may well be watching TV together or letting the other quietly read, but it may not.

There is real value in such structures as the Marriage Encounter dialogue when spouses set aside regular time to share and communicate. Any method the couple have to help communication is to be promoted. One couple had a brief sherry time before the evening meal, during which the children knew Mum and Dad were to be left to talk.

Husband and wife need time together. This is really precious, and I think many couples will agree that sometimes they should spend time together without the children, whether it be a short holiday or time when the children have gone to bed. Partners should discuss the balance between letting each other have due time for sport and relaxation, and spending time together. God cannot effectively work where the human side of things is out of balance. A married man and woman must find time, however briefly, to communicate as persons.

Sometimes this communication will need outside help from a trusted friend or counsellor. For heaven's sake, do not neglect this source of help. Some partners say, 'It will work out. We don't need help'. We all need help sometimes. The unity and very life of your marriage may be at stake. Do not leave it too late. Sadly, stories that have come to me indicate that counselling help is sought when there is a very thin foundation left for unity and fidelity. I think it tragic to be told, 'The first question (the counsellor) asked was, "Do you want your marriage to continue?"' If the answer from either partner was, 'No', the topic suddenly became, 'How to break up peacefully'. Choose your counsellor carefully. Get help in early days.

I am very impressed by my niece and her husband who used marriage counselling before marriage, some months afterwards, then to help with the new relationships caused by the arrival of their first child, and they probably will at other times, too. Such additional help to their own communication has become normal. Their relationship with

the counsellor is good and it is unnecessary to explain a
lot of background each time they meet.

Sometimes a couple's communication will lead to prayer
united with Jesus' prayer. The more they desire to enrich
the meaning and value of their lives, the more will they
desire this communication with each other and with God.
It is because God is the best and most sensitive communi-
cator that the couple needs to bring God into their relationship by prayer.

God is at work through the partners' unity and fidelity
to bind them together for their own sake, but also to
show all people the effects of God's presence and Love.
The fidelity of God's Love is revealed to us through the
couple.

> Let married people be united together in equal affection
> [so they] will bear witness by their faithful love . . . to that
> mystery of love which the Lord revealed to the world (52,7).

Here is the purpose of God being at work through the
love of the spouses and in Christian marriage: to reveal
God's Love for us. I am struck by the opinion I once heard
that the level of God's Love in the world is measured by
the level of love present in marriage and family life. Marriage
and family are like a thermometer of God's Love.

This is not to condemn partners who have decided to
separate or whose marriages are broken, implying that God
did not or does not work through them. In fact, I am sure
God works through them in a special way. I am stating that
those Christian couples who have decided to remain
together, despite difficulties, 'for better or worse', may give
clear evidence of the unifying and faithful Love of God.

ACTION

Unity does not always come easily but must be worked out. What positive steps can we take to promote unity in:

(i) Our relationship with God?

(ii) Our relationship with each other?

(iii) Our relationship with our family?

5. THE SEXUALITY
OF HUSBAND AND WIFE

• EXPERIENCE

'The best sex lives going'

'Christians ought to have the best sex lives going.' That is
how Richard summed it up, in a sharing on sexuality and
marriage. 'Marriage and sexuality are dear to God's heart.
God wants us to experience the fullness of it,' his wife Val
added. 'Sexuality is good and holy and we are meant to enjoy
being men and women,' they stated. 'God has planned
married sexuality for us in a positive way. The holiness of
sex is best appreciated by entering into it and enjoying it.
With God's plan and blessing for us it's clear we ought to
have the best sex lives of all!'

Some healthy attitudes to married sexuality expressed by
couples were: 'Sexuality is the highest expression of our love
for each other. It is involved in all our love.' 'We share peace,
serenity and comfort through our sexual relationship, a
reflection of our joy in knowing God and God's goodness.'
'God heals strained relationships, giving us an opportunity
for an outflow of love.' 'God has given us each other and
that makes us sensitive to each other's feelings and moods.'
'God is present in the unity or oneness that is the harmony
of man and woman.'

'Our married sexuality needs a light touch and the ability
to smile at ourselves,' said Tom. 'We all "get sex wrong"
from time to time. The telephone rings; the kids interrupt.
You know what I mean. There's so much pressure "to get
it right", to "perform" with perfect techniques as a couple,
to achieve a "multi-orgasmic lifestyle!" Often that is centred

on self, what you can "get out of it", and not on loving surrender, acceptance and giving. Esther and I realised this again the other day when we were "doing some research" on sex technique. All was well until I fell out of bed! We both laughed. There was not much else to do.'

Sublime yet not simple

Sam and Judy outlined some of the joy God brings in their married sexuality. 'God works through the peace and joy married sexual relationship brings to us,' they said. 'We thank God for the joy of sex and the terrific physical and mental pleasure of married love. Being aware of each other's desires, sexual intercourse becomes a personal and spiritual as well as sexual relationship.'

'A successful sexual relationship in marriage means developing mutual trust in all areas of marriage,' stated Sarah. 'Foreplay is more than kissing and caressing; it is not just a physical activity. All the listening, consideration, openness, forgiveness, showing affection, positive attitude and affirmation that takes place through the day and week set the scene for a deeply personal sex relationship in bed. They say "I am cared for by this person". We need to choose to love each other all day; a choice to say something positive, to care for our appearance, to make time together, to give each other a hug. Sadly, the need for this is most obvious when mutual trust has been lost or is jaded. Then, as in other areas of marriage, it may be most sensible to get help from a counsellor or a third person both accept.'

So, while married sexuality has its sublime moments, it is not always simple to live out positively. As one couple stated bluntly, 'Frankly, sex can be quite likely to disrupt

our marriage. It's not easy to really understand the different
biological needs that Les and I have. Nor to reconcile these
with other needs, for example, the moral teaching of the
Church. Also a lot of literature today can be stimulating
but pushing you to flout Christian laws.'

• SPIRITUAL REFLECTION

God's blessing on human sexuality

(I would like to clarify how I use various terms about
sexuality. 'Sexuality' means the masculinity and feminity
of a man or woman. 'Married sexuality', or 'married love'
is the general sexual relationship of a husband and wife.
I use 'sex' to talk of sexual intercourse by husband and wife.)
Scripture gives us the basis for a very positive teaching on
sexuality and marriage. It is quite clear God blesses human
and married sexuality. The Word of God invites couples
to delight in their love for each other. For example,

> Yahweh God fashioned the rib he had taken from the man
> into a woman, and brought her to the man. And the man
> said:
> 'This one at last
> is bone of my bones,
> and flesh of my flesh!
> She is to be called Woman,
> because she was taken from Man'.
> This is why a man leaves his father and mother and
> becomes attached to his wife and they become one flesh
> (Gen 2:22-24).

This process of seeking personal unity is sustained by
such images as the First Testament presents when it
considers the wife as precious as water in the desert:

May your fountain-head be blessed!
Find joy with the wife you married in your youth
(Prov 5:18).

The rich love poetry of the Song of Songs leaves little doubt that God blesses the romance of love:

Let him kiss me with the kisses of his mouth.
For your lovemaking is sweeter than wine,
Delicate is the fragrance of your perfume.
  Your name is an oil poured out
  and that is why girls love you. . .
My love is mine and I am his. . .
  How beautiful you are, how charming
  my love, my delight!. . .
Set me like a seal on your heart. . .
  For love is strong as Death. . .
The flash of it is a flash of fire,
  a flame of Yahweh himself.
Love no flood can quench,
  No torrents drown
(Song 1:1-3; 2:16; 7:8; 8:6f.).

God works through both general and physical sexuality in the married couple's life. Regarding sexuality in general, God helps the couple bring their masculinity and feminity towards full harmony in intimate partnership. Together they promote those qualities which will ensure they will be a good husband and wife, father and mother.

God is present in the goodness that is the physical side of their sex life, too. Here again this can be best understood and unified when we reflect that married sexuality is part of the make-up of the person.

Married love is an eminently human love because it is an affection between two persons rooted in the will and it embraces the good of the whole person (49,1).

Married sexuality is a personal quality. Note the force of the words that married love is 'rooted in the will' and that it embraces the 'good of the whole person'. Married sexuality is not to be confused with feeling on its own, or lack of responsible decision. This type of married love 'is a far cry from mere erotic attraction, which is pursued in selfishness and soon fades away' (49,1).

There are times you do not feel like loving, but are committed to love. Here God comes to work in helping your will come into play and say, 'I want to love'. Married love is a positive value. God is at work to accept and confirm human sexuality as a means to support and develop the spouses' love for each other.

> Married love is uniquely expressed and perfected by the exercise of the acts proper to marriage. Hence the acts in marriage by which the intimate and chaste union of the spouses takes place are noble and honourable. The truly human performance of these acts fosters the self-giving they signify and enriches the spouses in joy and gratitude (49,2).

This is without doubt a beautiful passage. By being present, God reminds the couple of the value of sexual love. By recognising God's presence, couples make sexual intercourse truly personal.

This is very positive. Sexual intercourse in marriage is not merely condoned; it is encouraged as a source of joy and gratitude, of noble and honourable relationship. Any suspicion or diffidence regarding married sexuality is removed. Sex is an important gift to the partners. Married intercourse is morally good and has its own special dignity as an expression of genuine love. As such it enriches the married couple. It is a means to maintain their mutual love.

Sex is the most intimate expression of love and self-sharing. God wants to enter into that intimacy. The couple needs to invite God into their relationship to help. God is also at work blessing married sexuality in spite of the difficulties that can exist. By inviting God to be part of their relationship, married partners are helped to avoid abusing or taking the other partner for granted. It may help to recall that we experience intimacy without sex. We do not need physical sexual intercourse to live out married sexuality in a loving, intimate way. There will be times when a couple cannot have sex, but continue to grow in intimacy.

Because of Jesus Christ's presence, sex is made a sacrament of personal, Christian love. Married love is 'expressed' by sex which 'fosters the self-giving (it signifies)' (49,2). Married sex is a sign of love, but it brings love about, too.

Joy and gratitude

The effect of the awareness of God's presence in the couple's married sexuality is that the spouses are enriched 'in joy and gratitude' (49,2). God will ensure full humanness in the partner's married sexual relationship. Such humanness will bring reciprocal joy and satisfaction to the couple. Indeed, they will each be concerned to seek the other's enrichment.

We are certainly not speaking of a sentimental joy, or implying that every sex act is going to be full of perfect joy and satisfaction. Married love, expressed in a form of sex that seeks the good of the other, will bring true joy and grounds for gratitude. Part of the condition for this discovery of joy is chastity. Chastity needs to be presented in a positive way. As Christians, we have to show that chastity is the better way! Chastity is a positive help to be an integrated sexual person.

Chastity directs a person's sexuality according to their state in life. Married chastity will ensure partners use their married sexuality to foster their love and growth and that its expression be tender, affectionate, personal and reciprocal. Hence we find married and engaged couples are exhorted to nourish and foster their lives with 'chaste love' (49,1) and the sex union of couples is described as 'intimate and chaste' (49,2).

> All this is possible [harmonising married love with the responsible transmission of life] only if the virtue of married chastity is seriously practised (51,3).

Chastity brings self-control and moderation of the sex drive for the true good of the couple. Married chastity helps make sure neither partner uses the other as some 'object' merely for selfish pleasure. It brings true intimacy and tenderness to sex because it makes it personal.

Thus the sexual relationship of husband and wife, and especially sexual intercourse, is blessed by God. God works through the spouses as persons in a human and pleasurable way. God pours out personal and spiritual riches on the couple to their joy and gratitude, in order to demonstrate more of the nature of God's Love.

Difficulties in married sexuality

Let us not deny real difficulties in the relationship of married sexuality at times, nor the fact that, at other times, the feeling of joy and gratitude will be far from the couple or one of the spouses. Partners acknowledged real difficulty in this area.

That is what the Church is saying when it parallelled Jesus' own joy and suffering with that of the spouses and the link of the two in faithful love:

> [Married partners] will bear witness by their faithful love in the joys and sacrifices of their calling to that mystery of love which the Lord revealed to the world by his death and resurrection (52,7).

Sex can assist building unity in marriage. It can also be destructive. To make sex a unifying factor, needs sensitivity to how men and women are different in their thinking and approach to sex.

Couples need freedom to respond to each other sexually. This often entails being freed from the effects and personal bonding of other sexual relationships experienced prior to marriage. It is no use sidestepping these areas, as if they have no bearing on present lovemaking in marriage. Unless they are faced and dealt with, we automatically bring their influence into how we relate today.

Couples will know something needs to be sorted out because they will experience 'blockages' in their sex relationship. These may take the form of disinterest in sexual intercourse with their spouse, sex becoming mechanical, impotence (where this is not a physiological difficulty), failure to reach climax (again, if not physiological or phychological), memory flashbacks of other sex partners, and fantasy and preoccupation. It is important to get proper medical care for physiological difficulties with sex. So, too, to get psychological help for emotional blockages. This may entail professional counselling and support.

The need to get help is especially true for spouses who were molested or abused as children. Other causes of sex blockages are the negative attitude to sex our parents may have had, rape, homosexual relationships, premarital sex activity, and, for married people, extramarital sex relationships.

This is a delicate area which needs counselling help. A Christian counsellor and the couple themselves can invite God's forgiveness and healing Love into their lives. It is important to remember this is our problem and not just his or hers. Where a couple is aware of the cause of the blockage, prayer together is very effective. God's Love works through a couple ministering to each other, which will help free partners to begin to relate again with trust and love. This is often a slow process, but God works through spouses to build that trust and love. Sacramental reconciliation will help, too.

As a practical help, I have included in the ACTION section, a prayer that couples may decide to say together to help heal and free their married sexuality.

It may be painful to work through these relationships, and at times we may feel we are making no progress. However, God will help, and even surprise us, with the joy regained intimacy will bring. Our choice sets the pattern of married sexuality. God will honour that by a growth in love.

Natural Family Planning

Some couples find difficulty in appreciating Church teaching on Natural Family Planning and incorporating it into their love.

One day I went for a jog on the beach with Michael, a married man with several children. We had mentioned companionship and other issues about marriage, when he suddenly burst out with, 'If you can do anything to help couples with Natural Family Planning, it would be marvellous! I have really struggled to keep to Church teaching, but it's difficult. Any support you can offer would help, I'm sure.'

'Well,' I thought, 'as a priest and even moral theologian, I don't feel all that at home with this area of sexuality and family planning. It is, after all, married persons who are living it. They don't need some authority who is not the one facing the real personal cost of practising it make glib pronouncements. Celibates have no place in the married bedroom,' I argued. 'On the other hand, my own abstinence from intercourse does teach me a lot and it costs. I do have some basis for comment. I also need to call on the same God for the love to live my sexuality positively.'

Couples need help to appreciate why the Church teaches Natural Family Planning. They need motivation to incorporate Natural Family Planning into the love of their married life. Here is an area God has great potential to work in, providing a good human, personal foundation is laid. I hope the following helps.

It may be important to make a distinction. Some find Natural Family Planning relatively easy to use and do not have a lot of difficulty with it. Both partners are committed to making it work. They have been able to plan when to have a child and their abstinence time is not too long. If you are in this group, give thanks. Try to understand those who struggle with Natural Family Planning, and do all you can to listen and support them.

The other side of this division is that group which has difficulty following through the use of Natural Family Planning. You may need special help. What is said here may not be enough and you need to talk as individual couples to others. Choose those others well. They may include a doctor who is sensitive and committed to Natural Family Planning, not in some clinical way, but with personal understanding of your situation. You may need personal help to make moral decisions as a couple. Not necessarily a couple or priest who will urge you to do as you please, but someone who will help you discern your situation before God and in the light of the guidelines of the Church. This will enable you to appreciate the benefits of living the values at stake. A Natural Family Planning clinic will be a good help. It will provide a committed and trained Natural Family Planning teacher or couple, with time to relate to you and work through your symptoms.

So, what are some of these difficulties? Perhaps a key one is where one partner is not really convinced about Church teaching or the value of Natural Family Planning itself. There are also practical, physical difficulties such as a constantly irregular cycle. Then other hormonal imbalances or unclear mucus patterns cause frustration. There is the human stress of it all. Natural Family Planning may work clearly before children come, but with several young children, other difficulties are encountered. Getting up during the night to feed a baby or attend a sick child can leave parents rather exhausted, unable to make love, let alone know precisely and calmly when is the 'right' time for intercourse.

Some couples have gone to heroic lengths in abstinence. In as much as I can, I give you honour on behalf of the Church. I ask forgiveness for any ridicule you have been faced with. You motivate me to grow in love myself. Practically, you remind me and all involved in Natural

Family Planning to do all we can to improve the method and its presentation. The Church's concern to develop Natural Family Planning and support it is set out: 'Experts, in other sciences, particularly biology, medicine, social science and psychology (are urged) to clarify thoroughly the different conditions favouring the proper regulation of birth' (52,4).

I am sure you could add other difficulties: the stress of already having several children; wondering if it is all a waste of time when maybe God is not too concerned anyway; fear of pregnancy, especially for a mother who has difficulty carrying a child or in childbirth; concern in later years where a child could seem quite out of place with old parents; the time around menopause...

What are the values of Natural Family Planning? These begin at a human level. Natural Family Planning needs to be truly human or it cannot be the basis of a Christian ethic. Strangely, this humanness has more often been recognised by non-Christians and others than Catholics. Maybe the Catholics have first seen Natural Family Planning as some Church obstacle to their married love? The Church favours Natural Family Planning precisely because it has the potential to deepen the human love of husband and wife. It is in the naturalness of the method that there is a basic value. There is no medical, chemical or other intervention. Natural Family Planning rests on human decision and planning. The cost of that is that you need mature partners and truly human conditions for Natural Family Planning to work.

Another value of Natural Family Planning is that it depends on and builds up the relationship of husband and wife. I think it is fair to say Natural Family Planning will not work unless the relationship of husband and wife is one of realistic support and communication. Natural Family Planning can help a marriage grow strong.

It becomes a way of life. Behind this is the individual character building it brings about. Natural Family Planning brings the value of self-understanding. This gives people a freedom to choose and be in control of their own fertility. Not only does each partner have to face the background from which they themselves come (Did their parents use NFP? What attitude to NFP were they educated in?), but also each has to face themselves (Can I use NFP? Can I work in with my partner? Can I abstain from intercourse and find other ways to express my love in fertile times? Can I face myself and grow in this situation?).

Church teaching is based on the meaning of sexuality. Married sexuality implies an openness to love and life. It does not want to separate these deep truths, even in individual acts of intercourse. So, on the one hand, Church teaching does not approve In Vitro Fertilisation, which removes the physical bond of intercourse in the union of ovum and sperm, and on the other, does not approve of contraceptive intercourse, which closes off the possibility of life coming from a free and responsible act of making love in marriage.

In all this, a hidden value is often overlooked: the theology of the body. It is not simply a philosophical argument the Church makes. It involves being true to our nature as human, physical persons. Other issues of a more general nature come into it, too: the dignity of sexuality; the dignity of men and women themselves; the importance of married sexuality in their relationship.

Then there is the value of abstinence. My dentist emphasised this when I asked him about what should go into this book. One of the values he offered was that a couple should sometimes sleep separately, precisely to prepare for sleeping together as a conscious, fresh decision. He said this gave time for a deeper spiritual dimension to come into sexual intercourse. Viewed in this light, abstinence is another opportunity to experience God at work through mutual support and affection. The couple learns to give love to each other in ways other than sexual intercourse. They give for the person's sake, which will enhance their eventual giving in sexual intercourse, too.

Such personal values are essential, not just to permit God's working in the spouse's married sexuality, but for the proper functioning of Natural Family Planning. With the deep respect for each other and the loving affection that married chastity promotes, a couple will be better able to plan their family naturally.

Natural Family Planning needs good motivation and strong support systems. We have spoken of the essential support partners need to give one another. Also, the need of medical help that is sensitive, Christian and open to Natural Family Planning. An invaluable support is a teacher or couple trained in Natural Family Planning. They can build a relationship with the couple working at Natural Family Planning. That human, woman to woman, man to man, couple to couple support is life-giving.

Then there is the Christian support of other committed people. People who will love and give practical support in the years of childbearing, helping with younger children, helping motivate the couple so they see they are not alone. Support from the Church in its teaching and attitude and

practice towards married couples and their families. That
support will continue after a couple has had a family so
husband and wife are still treasured as persons.

Those are some points. I hope they help in your personal
situation and encourage you. Despite very real difficulties,
there is evidence that Natural Family Planning can be
a means of grace and God's working in married persons'
lives.

ACTION

(i) Do we need to grow in how we communicate with each
other about sexual intercourse? Share how you think
things have changed over the years for you and what
you would like for the future.

(ii) How do you feel about the following statements?
(Circle your answer and later compare notes with your
partner.)

A	B	C	D	E	F
strongly	somewhat	slightly	slightly	somewhat	strongly
disagree	disagree	disagree	agree	agree	agree

We have intercourse too often.

A	B	C	D	E	F

I am satisfied with our foreplay.

A	B	C	D	E	F

There are some aspects of our married sexual
relationship that I would like to change.

A	B	C	D	E	F

Our marriage relationship is romantic enough.

A   B   C   D   E   F

You may want to share the answers with each other and discuss ways of enriching your married sexuality.

(iii) The following prayer may help you to pray together as partners to bring healing to your sexual relationship:

God, you created us and gave us to each other. I thank you for the gift of (name), who is precious in your sight. I love (name). May our love be a source of healing for each other. May your Love break any sexual attachment we may have formed with another person by wrong thoughts, words or actions. We desire to be completely one in and through you. We ask this in the Name of Jesus. Amen.

6. THE DAILY LIFE OF COUPLES

• EXPERIENCE

'Just go home and love'

One lady cheerfully asked me at a meeting, 'What are you doing here in Kilkenny?' 'Writing on God at work in Christian Marriage,' I said. 'Oh,' she replied, 'we've proved that for forty years!' It was my turn to say, 'Oh!' 'Well, where does God work in your marriage?' 'Everywhere,' she proclaimed without hesitation. It was an encouragement to me then, and maybe to you now. It was a lesson to me that God could surprise me in the midst of my day.

'You know, I'm sure it's in so-called small things that God's Love transforms our life,' Kathleen explained to us. 'I mean the dishes, cleaning, washing. These often lead to very important things. My husband, Nick, began talking to our neighbour about his vegetable garden and this gradually led to a whole friendship that helped save our neighbours' marriage. It is not so much "doing your bit", but making love your life in everything,' Kathleen summarised.

Another life-story illustrates how we need God to speak to us in the ordinary events of each day: 'It's amazing what can be learnt at the clothes line,' Veronica shared with the couples at the Teams' Meeting. 'When we were first married, Peter would be so helpful and peg all the washing out. The only trouble was I felt he had done it the wrong way, so would go out and re-peg it! You can imagine we needed to sort that out.

Then, one day, our neighbour came in and was chatting while I set up the washing. "Oh, you don't separate all the whites?" Well, no, not if it's a small wash. "You don't hang the shirts and blouses on separate hangers?" Well, no! "You use only cold water?" Yes, as a matter of fact, I do. This daily task had become a potential mine field for judgments, or feelings of anger or inferiority.'

It is in daily areas like this that God can be very much at work. You could think of your own stories.

Now we have a clue where to begin to tap into God's Love at work in the love of husband and wife. It is too much to say 'I must renew the whole of my married life'. We can begin at the daily level. Perhaps the secret is revealed in the words of one spouse, 'Just go home and love'.

- SPIRITUAL REFLECTION

The Love of God transforms all the couple does

God is at work through all the couple does. God is at work through the partners' love, in personal affection and sexuality, in their children, and through community and civil society (52,2). God is at work through the persons the partners meet and work with, their own daily work and health — through everything!

> [Spouses] become conscious of their unity and experience it more deeply from day to day (48,1).

The Love of God pervades the couple's whole life. Hence the use of words like 'penetrated', 'suffused' in the statement:

> Spouses are penetrated with the spirit of Christ and their whole life is suffused by faith, hope and charity (48,2).

Perhaps it is like that all-pervading consciousness someone has of a loved person. That person becomes the motive for all of life. It is much deeper than an infatuation or a passing feeling of love. In marriage, it transforms all the couple does. The Love of God through Jesus Christ abundantly blesses every day and every action of the partner. The whole of the life of married people is transformed 'caught up into divine love' (48,2).

This is the full significance of the words 'spouses therefore are fortified and, as it were, consecrated for the duties and dignities of their state' (48,2). God's presence strengthens them each day to love each other and to fulfil their role. God's presence in the whole of married life ensures maturity for each partner.

Most importantly, it means that it is **through** marriage that they will find all they need for their personal perfection and their eternal salvation. God shows the couple the way to holiness is through their marriage. They do not have to rely on extra work or prayers outside marriage for this, as though they lived in marriage, but God was found elsewhere. Husband and wife complete their mission as persons and Christians in their married and family life. They have ample scope to perfect themselves **in** marriage. Spouses slowly appreciate that their daily joys and difficulties, responsibility, struggle to forgive and to give of self, to understand and to be patient, to suffer and to love, are all that is needed to sanctify themselves.

Daily growth

It is a question of growth in appreciation of how God is at work through daily circumstances. A couple can do no better than take a day at a time, for it is only from 'day to day' (48,1) that they will grow in the consciousness of God's presence.

This daily growth requires living according to the 'spirit of Christ' (48,2). Through Christ's Spirit working each day, all within each day will be transformed more fully. We can take a step further, and say that God is at work through the love of the spouses, because of the Love of God.

The couple needs to grow in the life of Jesus Christ by deepening their love each day. This will bring them a richer, deeper relationship to the Holy Spirit and an increase of Love. Married love grows the more it is practised. 'They will eagerly practise a love. . .' (49,2); 'This love is actually developed and increased by the exercise of it' (49,1). So that is where we begin. Each day, married partners need to love.

ACTION

(i) Do we invite God to share our life together and reveal his presence in the ordinary events of daily life?

(ii) Why not ask God to lead and guide you in some daily way that comes to mind now?

2

GOD AT WORK THROUGH THE COMMUNITY OF THE FAMILY

1. God at work in the general family situation
2. God at work through parenting
3. God at work through the children

1. THE GENERAL FAMILY SITUATION

• EXPERIENCE

Families give life

Each of us needs to get in touch with the background of our own family life. This can teach us so much about how we react to people and situations today. As my dentist said, 'Unless a couple examines their childhood years, they will wonder at some of their behaviour with their partner. Often we repeat a childhood pattern in a relationship, for example, 'being nice in order to please (as we may have done with our parents), rather than being openly honest about some differences and relating as two mature people'.

I remember waking up to what family meant to me after my first ten months away from home. I wrote a long letter, full of new appreciation of Mum and Dad. This covered practical things like washing done, meals prepared, use of the car, as well as a deeper sense of the love I had experienced. Dad wrote back understandingly, talking of his own similar experience. A new relationship and a fuller sense of family began. I guess it was a bit like Jesus' own experience with his parents after he had exercised his somewhat impetuous independence when he stayed in the Temple (Lk 2:39-52).

You may like to pause at the end of this section to take time to reflect individually, and then sharing as a couple, on your family experience and how it affects your life.

I find the whole idea of 'family' really precious and life-giving. Maybe that is why people spend so much time sorting out their genealogy or family tree. I certainly gained new pride in my 'blood' looking up the relations in Scotland

and Ireland. Family is one of the most powerful forces in
our world. It can embrace persons in a religious family, like
the Society of Mary, where we call each other 'confrere',
or 'brother and sister', or the family of the Church, where
we are called to care for each other. It is why priests are
called 'father', taking the title from the Father of all families
(Eph 3:14f).

You will be familiar with the New Testament praise of
the 'family members' of the early Church community, which
says they were united in mind and soul, having no hesitation about sharing what they had (Acts 2:42-47 and 4:32-35).
Maybe you have also heard how Tertullian, an early
historian, in his Apology (I,39), summed up the family
spirit, saying, 'See how they love one another'.

Tertullian throws light on how this first Christian family
shared things, supporting the poor and burying them,
helping children without parents and people confined to
their homes, caring for shipwrecked sailors, miners, people
on islands and in prisons. I am not sure if your family is
called to help miners or bury the poor, but maybe it is asked
to help victims of shipwrecked marriages, children without
parents, born and unborn, immigrants of island people and
prisoners, all real works of mercy the family can do. As a
prison chaplain pointed out to us in the parish, 'Each
individual must adjust personally when released from
prison. Families can help by offering the love prisoners may
not have received in their own family'.

One principle that is dear to me is 'like helping like'. I
am convinced it is in a Family Network that families can
help other families. As Margherita and Frank shared, 'One
of the greatest supports in our family is the friendship we
have with two or three other families who share the same

values and have children in the same age-range as ours. It all started when three of us commenced working in teaching Christian doctrine together. Since then, it's grown and we do many things together'.

In all these experiences I found God at work in a Christian family sense to provide life and spiritual values, and support to live them out in a practical way.

• SPIRITUAL REFLECTION

God in each family

Family life is vital today. When we feel swamped by crowds and change, God will often work in a family kind of way. God is concerned to be present and active in each family because it is a key way to bring people to God.

> It must be said that true married love and the whole structure of family life which results from it, is directed to disposing the spouses to co-operate valiantly with the love of the Creator and Saviour, who through them will increase and enrich God's family from day to day (50,1).

God is at work in each family to build community. The couple become living instruments of God's action. In this cooperation is revealed the nobility of being parents. God has an essential place within the Christian family:

> [The benefits and ends God has endowed marriage with have] a very important bearing . . . on the personal development and eternal destiny of every member of the family and of the whole human race (48.1).

God is present inside each family to live and help each member to grow towards full eternal destiny. God ensures the unity and growth of family life as such. God's presence finds expression in the family doing things together when its members can. Occasionally, God works in a family by helping its members rediscover one another later on in life. Christian family members should never lose hope in God's desire to heal and reunite. Too often, sadly, we hear the remark at a funeral, 'Why did we wait till now to get together?' One of our practical resolutions might be to enjoy family life to the full when we are alive.

Because of the place it has in God's plan and Love, the family 'constitutes the basis of society' (52,2). One way God reaffirms that is by ensuring each family be the place 'where different generations come together and help one another grow wiser and harmonise the rights of individuals with other demands of social life (52,2). That is the mark of God's presence: life and loving harmony, where a person grows to be fully him or herself, always concerned to respect and love the other. Those who know how young and old help one another will appreciate the place each has in the family. We need think only of how, in general, grandparents get new life from grandchildren and how a grandparent at table changes everything for the family.

Whatever their particular circumstances, God desires to be present in each family to help them and to work with them.

Family to family

God is at work in the relationship of one family to another.

> Families will generously share their spiritual treasures with other families' (48,4).

Different families are bonded by the driving force of God's Love. The Church is meant to be a People who know and love one another. Families sharing their 'treasures', and getting to know other families, is one way to achieve this. It is not just material help that families can give each other. Families are the way God promotes spiritual growth, too. This could be in prayer or religious teaching, for example, by Family Bible Camps, or the sense of personal support one family offers another.

That God acts through one family to sustain and enrich other families is one of the most important pastoral teachings of the Church. We must ensure that families deepen friendships with other families and that family members become more aware of the full significance and scope of the relationship they have with other families.

For this reason, proper education for living our marriage and family life is vital:

> Various organisations, especially family associations, should set out by their programs of instruction and activity to strengthen young people and especially young married people, and to prepare them for family, social and apostolic life (52,6).

> It is the duty of parents and teachers to guide young people with prudent advice in the establishment of a family (52,1).

Part of this preparation is for the couple to start practical involvement with other families from the start. Every family needs this support. In turn, families need to let God work through them to influence and help other families. Families can organise some outing together, with shared games, different ones watching over the safety of children, children going home to stay with other ones.

God comes with Love to work in the general family circumstances. Members of the family will experience that Love in one another and together. Other people and families

will experience God's Love when they contact such a
Christian family.

ACTION

  (i) Sometimes couples or family members have difficulty
in sharing thoughts about each other with each other.
Many have found that writing down their thoughts
has been a help. Try completing the following
sentences and share them with one another:
- What I find most attractive about our family is. . .
- The most wonderful memory I have about our
family was when. . .
- I think that if I could change our family. . .

 (ii) As was suggested, you may like to take time to reflect
on your own family experience and how it affects your
life and family now.
Share with each other.

2. GOD AT WORK THROUGH PARENTING

• EXPERIENCE

Being valuable as parents

I remember one of my teachers giving me a good lesson about being valuable. He was a University lecturer at the time, and he used to get very involved round campus. A visitor came looking for him and tried here and there for a long while. 'Where on earth were you?', he burst out when at last he cornered him. 'I was being available to my students,' was the reply. 'It's no use being available, if you are not valuable,' was the quiet rejoinder.

Parents have unique value. Nothing can replace that. Parents, like my teacher, need to be both available and valuable. The children I meet reveal so much about their parents and the value of the upbringing they have had. For example, little Roberta, about six, came up to me the other day and gave me a big hug. Admittedly, it was round my knees, she is so small, but it told me a lot of what her parents have taught her about signs of affection. It was life-giving.

Her father, Thomas, indicated something of the spiritual and human background he and his wife, Gerda, have. 'We believe we share in God's Love when we helped create and now do our best to bring up Roberta and Nicholas. We try to guide them wisely, but we're ready to learn from them. We laugh together and share our joys and sorrows openly as a family. We begin to help them form their consciences by answering their questions as clearly as possible, admitting when we are wrong. We try to be honest with each other as the basis of family trust. We communicate as best we

can. We feel if we can give them security here in a loving
family, they will grow up with faith in themselves.' I think
Thomas' theory is working. At least Roberta's hug felt that
way.

Parents need to keep themselves valuable. You will think
of ways to do this. In parish life small support groups really
make a difference. Something personal like that could be
invaluable for parents. One couple I know visits another
Christian couple each fortnight to share and pray over
things. 'These very relaxed gatherings have worked wonders
for all four of us and are a real blessing,' they tell me. Just
as well, for their son recently made up his mind to leave
home because of his parents' attitude to one of his girl-
friends. This really tested their love for each other, for him,
and their trust in God. 'I don't know if Phillip has learnt
anything, but I can confirm that Dorothy and I have learned
more about parenting this year than in the last twenty!'

To grow in value and to get in touch with God's help,
spouses need time together. As parents they must not get
so caught up in meetings and other business that they are
not able to be present to each other and their children.
While parents can be concerned to help others, it is no use
being the perfect parent of everyone else's child. To be
valuable, the couple needs to 'practise an affectionate sharing
of thought and common deliberation' (52,1). This will be
completed when God is allowed to be at the centre of it all.

Mum and Dad!

'One of the things we've discovered is how important it is
to work in together,' explained Reudi. 'I take a share with
cooking when Ritta has afternoon classes. Our teamwork

involves the children, too. Each has a part to play, even the youngest. We help each other. In fact we've got a system that prepares as much as possible the night before.' Each family and set of parents can share something of that cooperation.

Parents need to create time together. Today parents can be swamped: driving children to and from sports, gym, ballet or whatever, women's and men's groups, parent/school Associations, civic meetings, Church meetings, business or work get-togethers . . . add your own! All this activity has to be countered by space for parents to catch up with each other and to ensure quality time with the children, too.

The Love of God can help parents be good parents, especially if both call on God's presence and help together. Marcel and Teresa are in the Charismatic Renewal. 'We have found a new peace and unity through the shared Love of Jesus. We used to fight and quarrel. We used to claim rights and authority and really end up being divided. We still have our difficulties. We went through a hard patch when I was the only one in Renewal, but now we have a new power to love. We can witness together to unity. This brings peace to the family and those around us. We had an overly-fervent stage, but that has levelled out. We still need more joy and tolerance, but we feel free. As well as seeing ourselves as husband and wife, as Mum and Dad, we see each other as brother and sister in the Lord. We have a unity in the Spirit that frees us to make best use of our differences.'

Some delightful moments can happen for parents. One creative father started taking his six-week-old baby son 'skiing' with him in the shower! He rides him on his thigh and they have a great time! What a lucky father and son. Andrea gives another example. 'I feel God is at work when

I talk to my three-year-old son, Justin. I chat with him as I peg out the washing. We thank Jesus for a flower or the sun and wind. We ask God to help Dad at work.'

Another parent experiences help in the sheer constancy of life, in the tiredness and stress. 'I don't pray formally. I just talk to God: "Please let the baby sleep", "Thanks for the day", or just, "**help!**"'

Some parents arrange space so they can do some work at home for necessary income. This enables them to stay close to their children. One arranged for her child to spend nine till three, three days a week, with a mother of another culture, who was minding her own children as well. This provided needed support for that mother and her family, and a cross-cultural experience for her child. Living in a multicultural city, the parents hoped their child would grow up to accept and respect persons of different cultures. At this stage it was a more personal alternative to a larger creche. It meant, too, that the mother could get a respite for herself and her homework, and be refreshed to be a truly loving wife and mother.

Mary, mother of Jesus, can be a challenge to us today. Part of that challenge is getting to know the real woman Mary is. One woman found it very difficult to get beyond the rather untouchable statue image she had of Mary. 'So, one day,' she recounted, 'I sat on a bench and told her directly, "I'm rather mad at you! You don't seem to be a real woman at all." Well, to my surprise, my outburst had some effect because I had a sense of Mary sitting down alongside me and saying, "Who do you think did a lot of the work around Nazareth? Who made sure there was something to eat when Jesus brought in all his playmates? Who worked with Joseph to teach Jesus?" Oh, I felt, she **is** real.

I've always tried to talk honestly with Mary and her Son since then.'

One man followed this up. 'Mary has a particular role in the family and especially the mother's life. I mean, it takes a woman to relate to a woman. I think we should adopt some more modern, Christian, title for Mary. How about "Mother of the Family"?'

• SPIRITUAL REFLECTION

Parents' way to God: interpreters of God's Love

We have seen how married love gives life to the couple themselves. Now we look at how that love finds life in children and parenting.

> Married couples should regard it as their proper mission to transmit human life and to educate their children. They should realise that they are thereby cooperating with the Love of God, the Creator, and are, in a certain sense, its interpreters (50,2).

This quotation sums up exactly what we are reflecting on. God is present as a loving God who cooperates or works through parents. Parents are interpreters of God's Love.

> [For parents to cooperate with God's Love] involves the fulfilment of their role with a sense of human and Christian responsibility and the formation of correct judgments through docile respect for God and common reflection and effort, consideration of their own good and the good of the children already born or yet to come... (50,2).

To let God really be at work through them, parents need docility. This openness to discover how God's Love works for them in practice will be the mark of Christian parents. Parents are the models for their children's future character. Being a model can be a bit frightening. Bringing up a family is not easy. For Christian parents, doing one's best to let God's Love come through to the children, will be a guaranteed way of success. Even in the most difficult cases, for example, when teenage problems may arise, being an interpreter of God's Love is a clear model. God's Love and forgiveness never cease.

Christian Marriage gives parents power to show that type of love. Parents could profitably reflect on Jesus Christ as the Good Shepherd who interprets God's Love by knowing and loving his sheep. 'I know (and love) my own and my own know me' (Jn 10:14).

It is important to understand the way God is at work. God works by using all the human elements which affect the family: temperament, economic situation and relationships with one another. Discerning what to do will mean reflection and effort by parents. God waits for an invitation before beginning to work. The family situation must be brought before God:

> It is the married couple themselves who must in the last analysis arrive at these judgments before God (50,2).

All this provides the parents' way to God. Once invited into parents' lives by prayer and reflection, God will work with them. Together they will set up a family community. The proper upbringing and education of a family provides all that is necessary for parents to grow in character and spiritual integrity. I have to spend only part of a day in a home with lively children to see that! Family life entered into with generosity and trust in God will provide parents with a sure way to meet God on earth and attain heaven.

Whenever Christian spouses in a spirit of sacrifice and trust in divine providence carry out their duties of procreation with generous human and Christian responsibility, they glorify the Creator and perfect themselves in Christ (50,2).

This does not mean some self-perfecting process. The couple lets Jesus Christ enter their marriage to perfect them. They are to cultivate trust in him.

Please stop and reflect on this. Otherwise, the sometimes frantic moments – when children are crying, busy about everything, tired and grizzly, bringing embarrassing feelings by their noise and behaviour in public, in Church, or before a visitor – can just remain simply humanly taxing times. A Christian outlook transforms such occasions with generosity and support. While these situations do not go away, God is present to help. A quick look to your partner will generally bring a sign of God's help, too. Usually one or other of you will be able to come to the rescue. Or, if it is really a tight corner, take time out together with some sign of support.

Special blessings will be needed by those parents who prudently and courageously have a larger family, with the heavier responsibility that comes with that generosity.

Among the married couples who thus fulfil their God-given mission, special mention should be made of those who, after prudent reflection and common decision, courageously undertake the proper upbringing of a large number of children (50,2).

A large number is not a set number, like seven or more children. Today, four is seen as a large family. The point is, God will work in a special way with parents who have a larger than average family.

Parents can take encouragement about how the Church describes their task in life. The idea of having a lofty role (48,2) as father and mother literally means they have a sublime work. We need to cultivate the respect and appreciation due to parents. Being an interpreter of God's Love as a parent is their way to God.

Cooperation as Father and Mother

God will help parents to cooperate in a spirit of accord and affection. This cooperation will provide the normally balanced atmosphere needed for a child to develop properly in security and joy. God helps the couple agree on the basics of forming their children.

> The married couple must practice an affectionate sharing of thought and common deliberation as well as eager cooperation as parents in the children's upbringing (52,1).

The basis of God working through the community of the family is the unity of love God has established between the partners. They must continue to share and consult with each other, and agree on a mutual life of education of the children. God will help with this. We know how quickly a child can sense disunity and will play off one parent against the other. If children do not experience unity in their parents, they will not see unity as a priority in their own lives. Hence, it is all the more important to let God enter in to deepen their cooperation as parents.

Husbands and wives are partners, working together. Even given that partnership, God works through them individually. We hear parents comment on how each of their children is different. So, God will work differently through the father and mother as parents.

God knows the 'active presence of the father is very important for (the children's) training' (52,1). The image of father will be set for much of the child's life, and how the child relates with their father will influence how s/he relates with other men. It is here the child will get a vital impression of God. A healthy image will help when the child comes to pray the prayer Jesus taught us, 'Our Father. . .'

The child who looks to their father as model and ideal must find there the necessary security and support, the guidance to know right from wrong, the assurance that their father will be there to help and that they are loved. God will help the father after work to lay aside his preoccupations and spend time with his family. God will help him value his children as a top priority in his life. The guideline is clear: the father is to have quality presence at home. He is to be actively present, playing, listening, disciplining, loving.

This will be helped if it begins with the father's presence at childbirth. This will bond him to his new daughter or son in a special way and there will be a renewed relationship with his wife. That bonding should be begun in pregnancy, with the father speaking to his unborn baby and by being a practical presence to his wife.

What about homes where the father or mother is not this model, is not present, or, when present, is not a good model, possibly being aggressive or drunk? God will enter this situation, too, and help the other partner find support and be able to supply the basic love their child needs. A good prayer for that parent is to ask God to fill in the gap between the love the child got and the love which s/he needs. That prayer could take place each day in their child's room and even more powerfully at Eucharist. I am talking about serious situations. There are lots of other times when the parents will show their humanness, losing patience, feeling angry or depressed. Parents and children can come to terms with this human face we all have, provided it is accompanied by sorrow, forgiveness and a new beginning.

God works through the uniqueness of the wife and mother, too. She has a 'central role in the home, especially (for) the younger children' (52,1). God is concerned about harmonising the 'woman's legitimate social advancement' (52,1) with the role she has as mother of her children. It is God first and foremost who gives value to the person of the wife and mother. The closer she relates to God, the more she will be fulfilled in marriage and in life itself. God at work in Christian Marriage means that it is a noble role to be a woman, and that childbearing and motherhood are precious and praiseworthy undertakings.

No-one can replace the mother in the home. The relationship she forms with the children, especially in the first years of life, is vital. All must be done to keep it intact. She should not be made to feel guilty if she is not earning money or doing lots of other things as well. After that, a harmony should be sought between the needs she has at home as mother and the needs she has in and outside the home as woman.

A woman has the right to be a mother. She also has the right to a career. It is interesting to note many women consider home-making their present occupation or career. So it is, and a noble one.

Running a home requires lots of energy and vast organisational and relationship skills. Some wives work part time inside or outside the home. This may be to help with needed family income, or simply be undertaken out of personal interest.

God wants to work through parents to ensure the fulfilment of the responsibility they have to relate to their children. God helps them cooperate with each other as mother and father both to serve their children and to find all they need for their personal and family lives.

ACTION

(i) 'Dear God,
You know what we are facing now in our job of parenting. Please help us to. .'
(How would we complete this letter?)

(ii) Parents are 'interpreters' of the Love of God in educating their children (50,2).

Are we as parents more interested in training our children in the way we think they should go, rather than the way God has planned uniquely for them?

3. GOD AT WORK
THROUGH CHILDREN

- EXPERIENCE

'Zeep-zeep-zeep-zeep-POW'!

'Children don't want our logic. They want us and our love.
They want to know we are real. How can we tell them to
go to Church, or be honest, or on time, if we don't feel it
is important ourselves. We must show love to one another,
not just talk about it.' Malcolm has captured something very
valuable. Parents' relationship with their children is to show
them love and live it out.

I cherish memories like that from home. Sunday supper
round our fireplace with Mum's toasted cheese sandwiches;
lying on the carpet, watching the flames, sensing the
warmth, conscious of the presence of Mum, Dad, my sister
and any visitor we had. What are some of your favourite
childhood memories?

Children conscious of this sort of love respond with love
for us. Mind you, we do not always have such positive
stories to tell of our children. Recently, Janet included
greetings from the family in a letter to me. 'I know Dennis
would want me to send his regards. The girls say "Hi".
Kevin is in disgrace in his bedroom, so I won't approach
him, since his comment may not be printable!'

God is ready to turn any situation into one where we can
learn something. Young Willie is a case in point. He is
intellectually disabled and a member of a larger family. He
loves to answer the phone and is quite happy to chat away.
He has high sensitivity and can feel trouble before anyone
has expressed it. 'If a couple of us get angry,' his father

explained to me, 'Willie will immediately come between us and cry out "No! No!" He plays up at times, too, but we wouldn't be the feeling family we are without his sensitivity.'

Another couple related how they had been trying to have a quiet prayer time with the children during Holy Week. Simon, their third child, got rather bored with this and went off. He returned with a noisy Space Gun. Zeep-zeep-zeep-zeep-POW! Nick, his quick-thinking father, said, 'Wow! That's just like a Prayer Bomb of the Holy Spirit!' So everyone had to be zapped: zeep-zeep-zeep-zeep-POW! May the Holy Spirit fall on you. Zeep-zeep-zeep-zeep-POW! I suspect the Holy Spirit enjoyed it all, too.

Some of the ways parents have described God at work in their children include: 'through prayer and love; talking about God together; caring for each other; forgiving; trusting; attending Church together, loving each other despite misunderstandings'.

Of course, children grow up and change. That is a time when it is sometimes hard to see God working through them. As Shona said, 'So many Mums come to me worried to death about the attitude of their teenagers, not only to religion, but to all sorts of things. I don't know what to advise, but urge them to keep the channels of communication open and to pray like billy-o!' Pretty good advice! The returns may not be too tangible at first, but love will win out.

Teenage attitudes and way of life are problem areas that tax Christian parents, like any loving parents. 'Did we go wrong? Were we too strict? Were we not strict enough?' They may bring feelings of guilt and frustration, and can be a real trial. One parent commented to me, 'Some of us are really confused and need help so badly. In our effort to be loving and non-judgmental when our children give up our moral code and religion or join some fringe group or live together, we feel like we are losing our own faith and balance of life. We try so hard to be loving and to understand and not lose our children, we end up wondering if marriage and other values are all that important. We wonder if the kids were right. We question things we previously had no doubts about. These are the times when Christian Marriage and the Love of God seem like a life raft to us. The best advice we can offer parents is, "Stay on board!"'

'One of the most moving moments of my own life, and probably our family's,' Gerard, a father and husband recalled, 'was when Eugene, our eldest, left home. It came sort of spontaneously, but I put my hand on his head and prayed for him and his safety in the future.'

Another father feels this very strongly. 'Parents have special power to pray for their children. We can put our hand on our children's head and bless them.' That taps into the teaching that any Christian has the power to bless and pray for someone. As a personal example, while I feel privileged to say the blessing before a meal at someone's home, the father or mother of the family whose house and home it is, seems to me to be the one who should normally bless God for the meal.

One family has an 'all-in' after that in which we can all say a prayer. Children's prayers, and certainly self-conscious teen's, can be rather mumbled, but also very telling. One, little Dianne, knew that Amen was the end and the signal to start to eat. At the first longer gap, she would make sure a loud **amen** echoed out!

'We'll remember you at candle time'

Lynn and Ron write, 'We have a prayer candle that is lit at the end of the evening meal, and placed in the middle of the family table. We pray for a short time, first with some set prayers, and then spontaneously. Paul, the youngest, blows the candle out, of course. A lot of things can be sorted out in that prayerful atmosphere.' I know the power of this family's prayer. Even though most of the children have grown up and some have children of their own, the love and prayer support of Ron and Lynn is still very real. Receiving a letter from them with a card signed by all the family was a great boost when I was studying in Rome, far from the fresh asparagus of home. 'We'll remember you at candle time.'

Families need time together to pray and be present to one another. Do you think it possible a parish could declare one night a week, a Family Night, and avoid all meetings on it? Everyone likes the theory, but I've yet to see it happen! In which case, let parents take their own decision and make their own Family Night. That night each will try to be home for the meal and to have some time together.

Some families have a Family Council, where each member can express feelings and make suggestions. Pat describes theirs: 'Everyone must listen and try to understand. At the end, we say a prayer. That prayer may be for healing or forgiveness, or for something we have planned.'

Sometimes, it is good for whole families to come together. Families can plan this sort of meeting for themselves. One of the happiest meetings I remember going to was the gathering of local Marriage Preparation Teams for whom I was Chaplain. We all gathered in one place. Parents met and discussed our program. Teenagers sometimes went together. Other times they organised games or special activities for the smaller children. They proved good carers of the babies. Then we would celebrate, singing at Eucharist. We finished with a meal together, a meal marked by much laughter. This was true family spirit and the evidence of God's work was clear.

In a similar way, the provision of a creche while parents attend something like a Marriage Renewal Weekend or Retreat Day is very practical. Do we use the opportunities Worship and Liturgy provide to involve families? One of the simplest, yet most graced and touching times of our parish Sunday worship, was a Blessing of Children after Communion, before the final prayer. The children would stream up from all corners of the Church, possibly bringing a smaller brother or sister, or carrying a baby or a doll or their Bible work, and line up for an individual blessing. It was a highlight for them and all of us.

I know for a fact that a children's sermon or shared homily, when children and young people take part, is really listened to. A little good companion who travels with me is a clown called Pippo. He has taught me a lot! He is a great asset as a visible teaching aid. Pippo says a word or two and the children, and their parents, are riveted.

This prayer and education helps both children and parents. I learnt this from Dad's last years alive. He got a lot of life from his children then. He could not proclaim strongly enough his gratitude for the material and spiritual help he received from family and in-laws. This ranged from prayer and letters, to ready-to-heat, deep-frozen meals prepared by my sister. In turn, we gained much from him. Perhaps his spirit is shown in that we discovered him getting out of bed to adjust the blind in the hospital the day before he died. 'What are you doing, Dad?' His reply showed much of the obvious thinking with which he tackled most things, 'I'm trying to live!'

While parents may look forward to their children growing up and being off their hands, the actual time they have with children is limited. You may like to make your own application of the advice one of my teachers gave me. I am certainly glad I followed it. He said to me, 'Make the most of your parents, while they are alive'.

• SPIRITUAL REFLECTION

Education through example and prayer

God's work in the family is two-way. God works through the parents to form the children. God also works through the sons and daughters of a family to influence their parents. We will unfold those steps a little now.

Getting the proper education for their children is a real concern for parents. Finding out what goes on at school and trying to keep track of television programs, videos, music, computer games and other influences on their children, is not easy. Yet, bringing up their children is an important consequence of being parents.

> 'When (spouses) are given the dignity and role of fatherhood and motherhood, they will eagerly carry out their duties of education, especially religious education, which primarily devolves on them' (48,3).

What words caught your eye? You do not feel too eager about it? You are probably not alone. Let us see what we can do. The text honours parents. They can justly take pride in the special place they have in family, Church and world.

The future rests on how you educate your children. We all need to promote the role of parent. Parents need practical help and consideration. You need time within your own families for this task. You need reassurance that you have the proper ability to achieve it.

Parents have a natural right to act as their children's educators. The more that can be done to help parents assist their child grow, the better. One area is preparation for religious seasons like Advent (Advent Wreath or Jesse Tree), Christmas (Christmas Crib, especially with the presents coming from the Crib) and Easter (an Easter Garden or Blessed Water). Then there are also special family events like a Baptism or First Communion. Other special times might be at meals, when children first go to school, pregnancy, birthdays or the death of someone known to the family.

God is at work through the parents to instruct and educate their sons and daughters in the things of God and to equip them for a fully human life. God will help the spouses set up an intimate community of life and love which is as fully human and Christian as possible. With this rich personal and spiritual focus, children 'will more easily set out upon the path of a truly human training, of salvation and of holiness' (48,3).

Here is a pattern of life and education for the family. God's working in the parents aims at this rounded education, one that is 'truly human' and yet truly spiritual, 'of salvation and of holiness' (48,3). Life in the Christian home should be human, with a place for things like hobbies, music, work, self-control, games, culture, reading, hygiene. It will be a lifestyle that places first things first: a religious spirit shown by religious symbols such as a crucifix, posters, candles, religious paper or magazine, Bible; whatever helps to remind us we are here for our salvation. Then the family should pray and go to religious services as a family wherever possible. All this is tied together by love. Love is the greatest educator of all.

Two practical areas where parents can further the education of their children with God's help are the example of Christian life and family prayer. These are keys in opening up a true family community. Just how family prayer should be arranged is something an individual family can decide. There is special power in the witness of wife and husband praying together. When they pray together, for example for a sick child, or over some family problem, there will be evidence of God's presence and power. 'For where two or three meet in my name, I am there among them' (Mt 18:20).

Children catch Christian values by breathing them in a Christian home from parents who have developed them in each other. One source here is the Word of God in Scriptures. Husband and wife could nourish each other with sharing texts or preparing the Sunday Gospel together. They could introduce the children to the Bible by stories or by reading a verse at table. Then a moment or two of shared prayer, however brief, before eating together.

Family prayer should be part of the Christian development of the family community. I think my own vocation to priesthood stems, at least in part, from hearing my mother and father praying together at night. The home is a normal place for God to work.

> It is imperative to give suitable and timely instruction to young people, above all in the heart of their own families (49,3).

The Latin for the phrase translated 'in the heart' (*in sinu*), literally means in the lap or fold of the family, its heart or innermost part, where there is affection and love. Much of the tone of education through example and prayer is set by that phrase.

Helping children establish their own life

Family education should include 'suitable and timely instruction . . . about the dignity of married love' (49,3) and preparation for a vocation in life, including a religious vocation (52,1).

'Suitable and timely instruction' includes sexual instruction. This is to be given in the context of love and wholesome chastity. Given at the heart of the Christian home, it could be better called education to love or family life education. Sexual education should be suitable, that is positive, insisting on sexual values, and prudent, not disturbing the sensibility of the child. It is to be timely, given when a child is ready for it and before ignorance would prove harmful. It is not so much instruction, or just imparting knowledge, as education, which positively forms a child to relate to others with respect and love in practice.

This education is also about 'the dignity of married love in its role and its exercise' (49,3). Children should observe the special place their parents' married love has in their personal and social life, including a healthy appreciation of sexuality. Because of this,

> If they marry, [the children] should be capable of setting up a family in favourable moral, social and economic circumstances. [In fact] it is the duty of parents and teachers to guide young people with prudent advice in the establishment of a family (52,1).

The best preparation for marriage and family life should be a person's own home. God is at work through the family community to see this happens. God will also sustain Christian couples in the sometimes difficult task of relating to their children. The Council has its own advice on the proper way to broach this general gap:

> [Parents'] interest should make young people listen to them eagerly; they should beware of exercising any undue influence, directly or indirectly, to force them into marriage, or compel them in their choice of partner (52,1).

In some cases, the parents may feel like using their influence to try to talk their son or daughter out of marrying someone. Here too, they cannot impose their point of view. They will probably get much further by loving, prudent advice and genuine interest. Meantime, of course, getting or losing quite a few grey hairs!

This is surely one area where God will support parents, especially in the heartbreaking event of seeing a son or daughter going their own way and perhaps dropping the practice of faith and evident Christian life. The feeling that comes after years of love and care is a confused 'How can they do that to us?' The constancy of parental love is needed then to wait and, in a non-judgmental way, witness to right paths, and keep loving and praying for their children. This demands more than human presence.

God is very present to such parents. God asks that they let their children go. Parents can expend endless energy praying for a child to come back to God or to a different moral lifestyle. I wonder if a lot of that energy should go into praying about other situations and be channelled into service of others. God knows the parents' prayer about their children and will act on it in good time. I often think of the parallel of an emergency in an aircraft. You know how the demonstration before takeoff says, 'Travellers with children should adjust their own oxygen mask first, and then look after the child'. I think some parents could do well to apply that spiritually.

One mother, who had a series of very difficult and heart-rending experiences with several of her children, shared with me that she had a sense of God telling her, 'Please leave them free now. I know your love and concern. I left you free. Surely, you can do no more than that for your own child!'

God may use these times to strengthen the couple's own relationship and support of one another. Parents need to be firm in standing by what they know is right and united in living out some truth together. Parents must never stop showing love to their children and offering a welcome to them. Truth and Love. God will work through that.

Parental education should allow the children to 'choose their state of life with full consciousness of responsibility' (52,1). One difficulty today for both young adult and parent is the difficulty of getting work at all. Ideally, children will adopt their own responsibility as adults and family people. With a proper use of their own freedom, they will see in life a task and mission, a feeling of being called to do something great and beautiful and follow their vocation in life.

There may be a lot of frustration and tension in the home as the transition from obedient child to responsible adult takes place. Later, parents need great humility, love, and trust in God to see their children set out in their chosen state of life. To discover that their children really are free persons can be a shock. It is a bit like the shock of discovering after years of knowing someone, including a partner, that he or she really is a separate person. True love will enhance that freedom. That love will enable parents to see that unless their child does make decisions s/he will never become a truly responsible adult and Christian. Parents can unconsciously hold onto their child with comments like: 'Of course, you will visit us', or 'You will get Simon baptised, won't you'. That does not leave much freedom or responsibility for their son or daughter.

Parents letting their children go is so important. The ability of a mother and father to do this can have a direct effect on whether their child can truly bond to a partner when it is time for marriage. If they have never left the influence of parents, it will be very hard to become *one* with a spouse. We may not realise the extent of the wisdom in the text: 'That is why a man leaves his father and mother and becomes attached to his wife and they become one flesh' (Gen 2:24). No leaving (or being freed to leave), then no real joining, no real becoming one body.

Further evidence of God's working in the area of education will be the parents and children's openness to their accepting a vocation as Priest or Minister, or religious Brother or Sister. This acceptance can occur because there is a Christian spirit in the family. The same argument would apply to their volunteering for work with people in developing countries.

Children and the family

Children have a special importance in God's plan and action in the family. This is illustrated by the fact that, in almost all marriages I surveyed in which parents have different

Christian religions or where there is a non-Christian married to a Christian, both parents feel they show God's Love to their children.

We noted that parents' interest 'should make young people listen to them eagerly' (52,1). Given that interest and love, God will call forth a willing and obedient response from the children. They will want to listen willingly to their parents. A simple formula, but a very powerful one. If parents want a positive response from their children, they need to show loving interest especially by the way they listen to them.

God's work through children is expressed:

> Children are the supreme gift of marriage and greatly contribute to the good of the parents themselves (50,1).

> Children, as living members of the family, contribute in their own way to the sanctification of their parents (48,4).

God uses children as active members of the family community to save the parents. Parents are encouraged to growth, generosity and openness when they see the same qualities in their children. Children are a source of grace for their parents who must develop many virtues in bringing them up, especially patience and love. To give to their children demands great sacrifice and will overcome selfishness. Perseverance will bring holiness and salvation to parents.

One of the special qualities needed in the relationship of parents and children is forgiveness. This is so important. It is a striking quality of God towards us while we are on earth. Therefore, we must show loving forgiveness to one another. 'Forgive us our sins, for we ourselves forgive each one who is in debt to us' (Lk 11:3f). As Paul writes regarding someone who 'has been the cause of pain' within the community: 'Now you should forgive and encourage them all the more, or they might be overwhelmed by the extent of their distress. That is why I urge you to give your love towards them definite expression' (2 Cor 2:5-8). Children really need that hug which says so much and restores that inner peace. So do we all, for that matter.

I have been struck by the number of spouses who cite: 'Never let the sun set on your anger' (Eph 4:26), as a guide for marriage. 'If there's a row, make up before the day is over.' Immediately after a disagreement may not be the time for an analysis of the situation. We need time to recognise our feelings and cool down. Nagging and constant pointed remarks do not help. However, before sleep, a simple 'I'm sorry', or a hug, or some sign of forgiveness, is truly Christian. It also means, humanly, that you are prepared to sort out some of the serious issues more openly the next day, or at some agreed time. It is important that children see this happen between their parents. It is human to have differences. It is Christian to forgive. God works in a special way through forgiveness.

God works through the children. They are to help their parents. One special time for this is when parents grow older or are sick.

> With sentiments of gratitude, affection and trust [children] will repay their parents for the benefits given to them and will come to their assistance as devoted children in times of hardship and in the loneliness of old age (48,4).

What a consolation this is for parents. It is also a clear guideline for all Christian children.

The effects of the place children have in a family extend into later life. Older parents and their children, who are now themselves parents, need to be sensitive to their relationship to each other. It can be very helpful for couples to meet again, say six months after marriage, with the minister or couple who prepared them, or some other counsellor, to see how things are going and explore their experience as children in their own family. One topic could be the relations with each other's parents. Nor should such a meeting be limited to six months after marriage, but it could take place at other times, too, for example to help adjust to a first child.

The coming of children triggers some complex reactions. The relationship these new parents had as children to their own parents surfaces. After an initial shock or sense of denial at experiencing again how they related to their own mother and father, new parents may need help to prevent any immaturity of relationship being projected on their own children. Maybe we unconsciously replay the model of parenting we know from our own experience.

Here we note:

> There should also be welfare legislation and provision of various kinds made for the protection and assistance of those who unfortunately have been deprived of the benefits of family life (52,2).

It is certainly praiseworthy to adopt or care for orphans and other children bereft of proper parental care. We should support parents and families with adopted children or children who have a disability. In an age when many would prevent such children being born, it is all the more striking that parents often strongly insist on the values brought to their families by those children. God can confound the 'wise' by working in such situations.

The Christian and the Christian couple have as their heritage the value of family spirit. It is not a question of formation programs, but rather a choice to let God and God's Love work through parents and children. As John summarised: 'My dear friends, let us love one another' (1 Jn 4:7).

ACTION

(i) 'Parents' interest should make young people listen to them eagerly' (52,1).
Over the next few days or week, try to observe the correlation between the interest you show in your child(ren) and their openness to you. You may be surprised.
Choose a time to evaluate this together afterwards.

(ii) 'Give a [child] a training suitable to their character, and, even when old, s/he will not go back on it' (Proverbs 22:6).
Discuss with your partner ways this training could occur given your family circumstances and the unique character of each of your children.
Possible areas to consider might be: family nights; shared family prayer; blessing at meals; reading; religious symbols and liturgies at home; discussing school; time with each child individually. . .

(iii) A Prayer you may like to pray together:
Dear God,
there are so many plans we have
for serving our children;
so many needs
to be met in each child
in so many ways.

We become overwhelmed at the enormity
of the task
and our own poverty.
Yet, we realise
it is only as You fill our spirits
and bring them to life
that we are able
to meet the spirits of our children
and respond to each
in a life-giving way.
Your Love
flowing through our earthen vessels
brings life.

Today,
we bring our children
and lay them in the midst of the house
in which You dwell
in Love,
Father, Son and Spirit.
May your Love,
the Love you have for one another in the Godhead
fill
our home
also.
Amen.

3

GOD AT WORK
IN MARRIAGE THROUGH
LOVE AND COMMUNITY

1. Love and community
2. God at work through Jesus Christ
3. God at work through the Holy Spirit
4. God at work through the family of the Church
5. God at work beyond the family

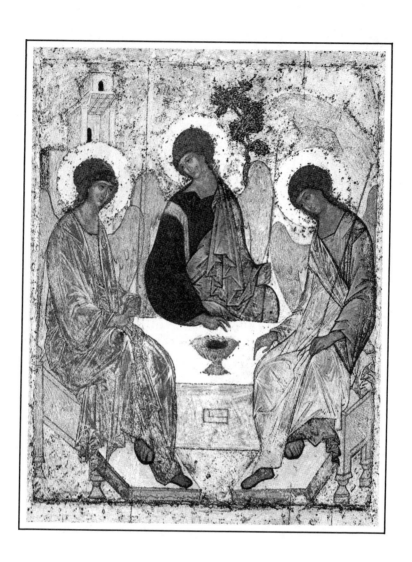

The Icon of the Trinity

The Greek work *Ikon* means a *living image*. Icons are a window into heaven, imaging and making present the living reality pictured. We need to contemplate and pray in the presence of an Icon to get drawn into that image and life ourselves.

I have chosen the Icon of the Trinity (*Andrei Rublev, Fifteenth Century*) to illustrate some of the elements of Love and Community in God. Here is a picture of God, which can be a powerful model for Christian Marriage and Family Life.

The three angels sitting at table are messengers of God who foreshadow God as a Trinity of three Persons: the Father at the left, Jesus in the centre and the Spirit on the right. The building behind on the left symbolises the Temple of God, the presence of God; the tree in the middle represents the Tree of Life, the Cross of Jesus, source of Life; the mountain on the right stands for God's Revelation, work of the Holy Spirit.

In the Icon are three distinct persons who are very much a unity. They resemble each other and yet, they are different. They are three and yet to take one of the figures out of the scene would destroy the whole rhythm of the Icon. The three are obviously communicating with a real sense of unity in diversity, and yet with a love that is totally open to others. We very soon feel part of the group, at home with them (Jn 14:23). The three are seated and yet there is obvious movement of communication, dialogue and relationship amongst them.

In your prayer I am sure you will discover much more. . .

1. LOVE AND COMMUNITY

- EXPERIENCE

Is the Love of God in the Trinity a model for Christian Marriage?

'I get angry when the Church tells me my marriage is meant to be like the Trinity. I'm a woman and I feel it difficult to relate to the male images of Father and Son. I've only recently sorted out something of my own relationship to my father, let alone sort it out with God the Father. I find other terms, like God meeting me in a nurturing way and in nature, help me as a woman, and I certainly experience that God in marriage,' Jo-anne stated bluntly. Her husband joined in. 'Certainly the Trinity is a head level concept. I'm not sure, but I think it's far above most couples. My experience of marriage is a much more down to earth one.'

Well, you can imagine my feeling when I heard all that! 'Do they know I am basing my book on the Trinity as a model for Christian Marriage? If Jesus has revealed God as his Father, surely there's something life-giving here? Is the Trinity "far above most couples"? If so, I thought, the book is sunk! Do I have to dodge that basis? Whew! Where to from here?'

As I took second wind I started to hear what was going on. Jo-anne had nothing against Church teaching or the Trinity in themselves. Like many women today, she was asserting the validity of a woman to express a feminine view point of relating. As she said, 'I've no objection to calling God "Father", and don't want to replace that by "Mother". However, I do feel as a woman, and that's part of my marriage.'

We are also faced by the fact that many women (and men) have a fairly negative experience of men in general and their father in particular. Unless this is addressed, a simple presentation of God as Father does not help.

Others have developed a positive view of the Trinity themselves. As Lorraine commented, 'I'm struck by the community nature of the Father, Son and Spirit. I find it a reassuring model that gives me an attainable plan from God for my marriage. It comforts me to live realising I am known by God in the depth of my being. That heals me, empowers me and brings me confidence to reach out further than myself. The freedom, equality and mutual understanding God's relationship has in the Trinity challenges me to relate to my husband in the same way. The example of the Trinity clears so much frustration and turmoil from the path of my life. There is now room for full life and joy.'

So the challenge faced me to explain the Trinity in a richer way beyond simply the terms of Father, Son and Spirit. Likewise, to go deeper than the head-level concept even the word, Trinity, evokes. I believe the Eastern Church's understanding, expressed in the Icon by Rublev on Hospitality and the Trinity, goes a long way to achieving that. It is reproduced so you can refer to it. The Eastern understanding is further outlined in the Spiritual Reflection section. Whatever our first reaction, the Trinity challenges us to stop and think.

The loving community of an open family

If God is really at work, the result will be shown in the family life people lead. One of the most delightful homes I visit is a type of open house — always very lively, with neighbours and children and friends coming and going, a house where a cut cake will normally disappear at one sitting! I remember visiting once when the mother was actually overdue for delivering a baby. Her first comment was, 'Hello, would you like a bed to stay here?'

There seems to be something about generous people. Their generosity knows no bounds. There is always room for another chair at table, a spare bunk to sleep on. I guess the proof of the Christian pudding is in the eating. Does it make us more human? Well, the home I have described is both very human and very Christian.

That is what God at work in love and community means. One sign of God's presence is a truly human family sense, a whole loving atmosphere where a person knows that they are loved. I am living in a home like that as I write this. We are a household of eight. Four of the main family, Mum and Dad and two children in their early twenties. Then, four household members, a nurse, a potter, a Malaysian student and myself. Add to this two boxer dogs who are always keen to go for a walk and one kitten, plus a fair share of visitors and you have a lively centre like the one described above. There is plenty of scope for consideration and team work as well as sharing of sadness and joy. Here is a school of learning: learning how to cope, how to balance privacy and community, how to respect culture and age and personality differences, learning how to love, forgive and love again.

Which is not to say we do not have trouble with butter in the honey or the shower mat left soaking on the floor! On the other hand, someone will point out and darn a hole in your pullover and all look forward to the Saturday evening Sabbath Thanksgiving Meal. God's Love is at work in a practical, caring family community.

• SPIRITUAL REFLECTION

In God's plan, Love is at the heart of marriage

God's Love is revealed in Christian Marriage in that God set up the basic plan to make marriage work.

[Marriage] has been established by the Creator and endowed by God with its proper laws. God is the author of marriage and has endowed it with various benefits and with various ends in view (48,1).

Marriage will work to the degree it follows God's plan. In this we see the loving design of God. God guarantees its stability. 'The divine law throws light on the meaning of married love, protects it and leads it to truly human fulfilment' (50,2).

God's Love is not an external appendix to marriage. God is at the heart of it. Our study of God at work could imply an operator working from outside. No! God's working is inside us. God's plan is revealed internally to husband and wife. Each partner will come to know God's Love for him or her. God's Love and forgiveness heals the past and sets each free to relate. God's peace and wisdom touches their present lives and brings perseverance and love into daily decisions. God's goodness and Love gives hope and promise for the future. God's plan helps each of the partners from within.

God's plan for marriage also has external guidelines and helps. This plan can be discovered in the Word of God. It is found in supportive people. Not least is the priest or minister who reassures the couple God loves them both. Ceremonies such as the renewal of marriage vows highlight this. These could take place in the home.

God's plan is not only a guide to be followed. God is a Person who loves partners and wants to work from inside at the heart of their marriage.

The Trinity unfolded

For Christians, God is Father, Word or Son, the Spirit, persons in whose names we are baptised. We call God a Trinity, three persons who live together, knowing and loving each other perfectly. The Father speaks as it were his word, his Son, and they know one another. God's life is not just knowing, but also loving. The very life or breathing of the Father and Son is Love, the Spirit of Love. The community of Father, Son and Spirit is a Community of knowledge and love. Jesus is the dear one, the loved Son of the Father who makes him known to us. 'It is the only Son, who is close (nearest) to the Father's heart, who has made him known' (Jn 1:18).

This is mirrored in Christian marriage. Partners are to know and love each other. God is at work in a marriage that is based on truth and love. Married love matures as partners learn the truth about each other and lovingly continue to accept one another. God works to ensure a married couple be thinking, loving persons. In this they are like God! They reflect the fact that men and women are made 'in the image of God' (Gen 1:27).

We have seen in the Experience section that the Trinity is not always the easiest to understand in itself, let alone apply to marriage as a model. You may like to refer back to the comments and illustration at the start of this chapter on the Icon of the Trinity.

Rublev portrays the meeting of Abraham and Sarah with Three Guests. That meeting is outlined in Genesis (18:1-15), if you wish to read it. Here we are given a warm picture of God, showing the richness of the three persons Jesus himself revealed to us: 'Father . . . I have made your name known to them' (Jn 17:25f); 'The Holy Spirit, whom the Father will send in my name. . .' (Jn 14:26).

There is an equality amongst the three persons shown in identical faces and staffs. There is a mutual understanding seen in the circle they form and in the movement of their eyes. There is a deep relationship with us, inviting us to come to table to share the cup of hospitality with them.

Here are some down to earth qualities with which married couples can identify. For example, hospitality. The dining table has a central role within a home. For Rublev, it was at the moment of hospitality offered by Abraham and Sarah that God was present. So God is especially present with a family as they share at the table where they eat together. The family table is a good place to start to see God at work.

God is Love and whenever God acts, Love is active. Father, Son and Spirit form the perfect Community of Love. There is an awesomeness when we think about God's own Love at work in Christian Marriage. The love of marriage is transformed with God's Love:

> Authentic married love is caught up into divine love. . . [Married love] rich in its various features [comes] from the spring of divine love (48,2).

The Trinity's Love is the source or spring of married love. There is a continued presence of God's Love in Christian marriage. The couple is 'caught up into divine love'. Married love is a sign of the presence of God's Love. Truly loving partners allow the Trinity to reveal this Love to each other and to those they meet.

Love is related to community in marriage and family

The relation of love to community in marriage and family takes full significance in the good news that God's Love has saved us. Through Jesus and the Spirit, God has freed us to love and build community. Christian marriage and family life, with its own tensions and demands, is a place where the action of God enables men and women to be free to love one another and relate in community.

Love is naturally related to community in that love builds community. Love creates union, bonding people together. Community in turn reflects that love; it is a loving place. Love is the heart of community. Love is the starting point for community because it frees us to be ourselves. Love frees us from fear, sin and selfishness, precisely so we can work with others to set up community. Without love there is no chance of lasting, healthy community.

Love is a starting point of married life, uniting the couple and building family. Love and community are related naturally. Marriage is referred to as a 'partnership of love' (47,1). This brings out the central nature of marriage and family: married love sets up community. The natural unity that arises from the love of husband and wife becomes a community of love and life stabilised by God.

The relationship of love to community becomes what Scripture describes as a covenant, a personal agreement. The personal consent of the couple becomes holy and a means of holiness (48). This Christian married love results in Christian community, or Church (50,1). There is the wider, social aspect too. The whole family, both the individual family and the family of the Church, loves others around it, inviting them to build and deepen Christian community.

The Love of the Community of God ensures the couple's love be totally for each other, uniting them totally. Married love becomes ever more genuine and rich because it is united to the source of all Love.

It is like the way of love St. Paul set down: 'I am going to put before you the best way of all' (1 Cor 12:31). This way is in fact the divine way of Love or charity which Paul develops (1 Cor 13). Love is a key way God is at work in Christian marriage. This way of Love is God's gift, God in our lives.

This does not mean a life of remote contemplation. The Love of God finds expression in daily life, in the love of husband and wife for each other, with all the qualities expressed in Paul's letter to the Corinthians (1 Cor 13:4ff): patient, kind, protecting, trusting, hoping, enduring, not storing up grievances, making allowances, unselfish, rejoicing in the truth.

ACTION

(i) How can we, as husband and wife, breathe life into each other?

(ii) What were the qualities I saw in my spouse that drew me to marry him/her? Do I still see these things as a gift of God's love to me?

(iii) We read about the community of Father, Son and
      Spirit knowing and loving one another with equality
      and mutual understanding.
      Discuss: Do we take time to know one another?
      Is there an unconditional love between us, enabling
      us to reveal ourselves to each other?
      Does each of us experience equality and mutual under-
      standing; that is, do I feel understood and that I under-
      stand my partner, especially in specific situations?
      Are there tools available to enhance our understanding
      of each other? What are these tools?

(iv) If we apply the words 'increasingly further their own
     perfection and their mutual satisfaction' (48,2) to our
     own marriage, can we make sense of them? In our
     circumstances and our struggles with one another, are
     we really helping each other to become more holy?

2. GOD AT WORK THROUGH JESUS CHRIST

- EXPERIENCE

Jesus' presence in marriage

One of the tests of a Christian Marriage is: does it work? That it can has been brought home to me by how couples live it out. From the outside it looks plain enough, but from the inside it is different. Different because God is present. This difference is often sharpened by Jesus' own presence. As Rosina told me: 'It's hard being a mother'. She did not need to elaborate on that as Rebekah kept dropping toys (and food) on to the floor and seemed especially restless this day with teeth coming through and all. Rosina went on, 'I believe God is present with me. I believe that when I see my children struggling or when life gets difficult. I don't really say a lot of prayers. I talk to Jesus round the house. I know God is with me. So I ask help for my husband, for each of the children every day and get on with what has to be done.'

It was clear to me the presence of Jesus in her and her husband's lives changes things. A bit like the way the marriage feast at Cana was transformed *before* the miracle of the wine by the very presence of Jesus and Mary! Jesus' presence changes ordinary things.

I discovered that from Jane's comment, 'I now do each thing, even cleaning the bottom of the saucepans, for Jesus!' and described how a consciousness of Jesus' presence had changed everything for her, even the dishes. It brought home to me the realisation that in truly Christian Marriage there is no such person as an ordinary housewife or ordinary couple. They are the salt of the earth people who do ordinary things with a fresh purpose. It encourages me to get the same out of life as they do.

This transformation can also take place at a much more serious level, that of fidelity. We live in an age when people witness widespread breakdown in marriage. Fidelity seems difficult to live out. Sad experiences between partners need a lot of healing. As one wife told me: 'I wanted to marry for ever. For me it's impossible now to live intimately for ever with someone, because my husband was unfaithful'.

That is serious, but it could be a turning point. Rather than giving up and possibly starting a whole lifetime that is isolated, their marriage could become stronger if the spouses can face each other honestly and talk it through. There is certainly a lot of hurt and a whole process involved in getting trust back, but a real facing of self and life can happen. If the truth can be spoken out and accepted, if forgiveness be asked and accepted, then a new beginning can take place.

'That happened for us,' Michelle shared. 'It was really painful and it took ages to come to terms with our relationship again. Our prayer and Jesus' presence helped us through. Now we are stronger and certainly wiser!'

I feel pretty humble listening to that. Maybe it will help you, if you have experienced the hurt of infidelity yourself.

Choosing Jesus as a couple

I am especially struck by the powerful force a couple makes when they have chosen Jesus together. I am saddened by a limping Christian Marriage, where there is not a strong choice of Jesus Christ. I am thinking of marriages where I have prepared the couple. The ones where the couple has chosen together to be committed to Jesus Christ stand out. Often a weak Catholic marries a baptised Christian of another faith. If the other Christian is strong in their faith, the Catholic may stir into some active Christian life. I am not trying to hurt those couples where one partner is a committed Christian, the other a non-believer. Often they live very fully and are remarkable for their witness.

My point is, how much more powerful is the marriage of two committed Christians. It is an uphill battle when I am preparing a couple who do not even know Jesus personally; who get angry because I suggest their coming back to church for the marriage day is only part of what it is all about; who never have really prayed together. From a Christian point of view, their marriage is weak from the start. It is not too late. Any initial choice of Jesus Christ is a beginning.

Made as a couple, the choice of Jesus Christ lasts, as Kay clearly told me. Her husband, Terry, had recently died and Kay wrote speaking of how the bond with him was still strong through the person of Jesus.

> The Scriptual meeting of Jesus with the two drifting disciples on the road to Emmaus (Lk 24:13-35) was quite a highlight for me. I could almost hear Terry sigh with exasperated relief when I got the message that every apparent ending is really a new beginning; that Jesus taught the disciples through Scripture and he revealed himself in the 'breaking of bread'. So now I know where I've got to go, how I get the instruction, and who I get the strength from.

Yes, it is in things like sharing the Word of God that a couple will find life. Ideally, in sharing Communion as well.

I am always moved when a couple comes to Communion and waits till each has taken the consecrated bread or wine and then receives together.

Mike summed it up: 'Once you've chosen Jesus as a couple, all the rest follows.' I fully agree. I invite you to make that choice now.

• SPIRITUAL REFLECTION

The presence of Jesus helps couples grow in love

Jesus enriches a marriage because he helps the couple grow in knowledge and love of each other and of God. Jesus makes the couple relate in a way more like his relationship to his Father. Jesus helps them accept each other lovingly. This loving relationship will be a lasting foundation for their marriage.

Relating like this does not happen by chance. Couples must be helped to know each other in the Lord. Each learns to build on the good points of the other and to continue that through life. It is beautifully summarised in Paul's prayer for the Philippians (1:9-11), which could be a prayer for married spouses or for all who help married couples:

> It is my prayer that your love for one another may grow more and more with the knowledge and complete understanding that will help you to come to true discernment, so that you will be innocent and free of any trace of guilt when the Day of Christ comes...

Jesus 'blesses' a couple's love; he 'abides' with them; he 'directs and enriches' their love; he 'helps and strengthens' them as parents; he 'fortifies and consecrates' them; he 'penetrates them with his spirit' (All from 48,2).

The presence of Jesus brings a richness to marriage it could not otherwise attain. Let us listen to the beauty and power of the text itself, which gives us a basis for a spirituality for married people:

> Fulfilling their conjugal and family roles by virtue of this Sacrament, spouses are penetrated with the spirit of Christ and their whole life is suffused by faith, hope and charity; thus they increasingly further their own perfection and their mutual sanctification and together they render glory to God (48,2).

The presence of Jesus Christ is essential for the spirituality of the spouses as a Christian married couple. It is this presence that makes married love the means for the couple to grow in perfection and able to render glory to God together.

This working of Jesus in the midst of the couple is a growing presence. Hence the deliberate use of the words 'they increasingly further their own perfection' (48,2).

This perfection as a couple lies in being united as persons Jesus unites. Jesus makes a couple better persons together. Jesus is not present as an observer. He actively helps partners' love become more authentic, more Christian. He personally accompanies them; he 'abides' with them (48,2). The text has the note of permanence, a continuing personal presence. It is an enduring presence, which the couple 'experience' more deeply from day to day (48,1).

It is a healthy reminder to see the basis of faithful love in the person of Jesus. Not only that, but Jesus is present in Christian marriage and brings that fidelity with him.

Jesus forms a covenant of love
with the couple

The key to Jesus' presence in Christian marriage is Baptism. Baptism sets up a covenant of God with a person and makes that person one of God's children. *A covenant is a personal agreement from the heart.* Baptism is the Love of God building up a people who are Church, people assembled as God's covenanted children. Jesus is present to incorporate Christian spouses further into the life they received in their Baptism. We could say Jesus redeems the couple. Jesus redeems them by freeing them from sin and all evil so they are free to love and be fully themselves. 'Authentic married love . . . is directed and enriched by the redemptive power of Christ' (48,2).

Jesus then transforms their love into a redeeming love. Being freed themselves, they can help free others. They are freer now in their love for one another. They will then free or redeem others, first in their own family and then more widely, touching those with whom they live and work. Jesus works through them in this freeing love.

> In the footsteps of Christ, the principle of life, (couples) will bear witness to and bring about that mystery of love which the Lord revealed to the world by his death and resurrection (52,7).

Couples need to become more aware of the presence of Jesus through prayer and reflection. Catholics call this presence in Christian Marriage a Sacrament, a sacred relationship or covenant. Jesus is present in the covenant of Christian Marriage.

> Just as of old God encountered his people with a covenant of love and fidelity, so our Saviour, the spouse of the

Church, now encounters Christian spouses through the Sacrament of marriage (48,2).

Scripture speaks of covenant:

I shall betroth you to myself for ever,
I shall betroth you
in uprightness and justice
and faithful love and tenderness (Hos 2:21).
I shall remember my covenant with you when you were
a girl and shall conclude a covenant with you that will
last for ever (Ezek 16:60).

Scripture takes that image a step further and sees a parallel between three sets of Covenant: the Covenant between God and God's people; the Covenant between Jesus Christ and God's covenanted people, the Church; the Covenant of Christian Marriage between husband and wife.

The jealousy that I feel for you is, you see, God's own jealousy. I give you all in marriage to a single husband, a virgin pure for presentation to Christ (2 Cor 11:2).

The Word of God even sees in the Covenant of marriage an image of heaven and Jesus' completed relationship to his Father.

Let us be glad and joyful and give glory to God, because this is the time for the marriage of the Lamb (Rev 19:7).

Jesus is present when one partner is not a Christian, or even if both are not baptised Christians. This is because something of the Love of God and God's Covenant is present in all marriages. Where Love is, Jesus is present and God is at work. The life and Love of God can still be present. This could be the beginning of a couple's more explicit knowledge of God as a Person.

In ministering Marriage to each other, Christian couples meet the person of Jesus. Far from being the receiving of something, Christian Marriage is an active meeting of persons. It is a new covenant or meeting with God through the person of Jesus.

This presence of Jesus is not just for life on earth. Covenant with God is for keeps. As the text tells us, the plan of God has 'a very important bearing on the . . . eternal destiny of every member of the family' (48,1).

Living out married spirituality with Jesus

The presence of Jesus with a couple makes their married love a means to grow spiritually. Just as God fully entered human nature when God became human in Jesus (called the Incarnation), so Jesus enters Christian marriage and makes a couple's human love holy from within. The married couple becomes the human vehicle to help each grow in the Love of Jesus.

Living out Christian Marriage does not happen by magic. Jesus enters Christian marriage not to wave a wand. Jesus empowers the couple to become fully themselves as human persons and partners. This process of becoming fully themselves is what spirituality or holiness is.

Jesus is present in the joys, difficulties, sufferings and happiness that come in marriage. Jesus works in a human way as well as spiritually. Couples have to be convinced of the unity of Jesus' presence in the wholeness of their lives. Whether only the couple is together, or the family is at prayer, whether we are experiencing some form of suffering or participating in those everyday events of eating, talking, working, growing in relationship, whatever − Jesus is present and the whole becomes more Christian, more human. The human becomes a sign of something sacred.

Living out married love is what counts. This is true spiritual holiness. The couple is to live married and family life according to the spirit of Jesus. Marriage is not just a celebration that took place on the wedding day. Marriage is an ongoing reality which enables Jesus to be present every day of partners' lives. Spouses need to pray to Jesus and God to appreciate this aspect of the spirituality of Christian Marriage and call on God whenever they are in need.

We arrive at a complete notion of holiness. Holiness is a giving of self, a love of the other, in this case, the other spouse. This is a quality that leads the couple together on the path to wholeness.

Holiness for the Christian couple is Christ-filled life and love as husband and wife, mother and father. Of course, holiness is also union with God for God's glory. 'Together they render glory to God' (48,2). I believe we should rekindle deep respect for Christian Marriage. Marriage is to be appreciated because it leads to the full spiritual health of spouses.

This appreciation or reference should continue in daily life. Couples are challenged to maintain this specialness of marriage. Husband and wife could well reflect on when they last did or said something to enhance the respect their love for each other and the children needs.

Spiritual holiness is a shared, daily way of life. '[The partners] increasingly further their own perfection' (48,2). It is interesting to note the term: their own perfection. Couples do not arrive at full perfection. We are not aiming at achieving some remote perfection portrayed in some advertisements, as though holiness were to be aligned with the perfect marriage or the perfectly spotless kitchen. The spiritual holiness which Christian marriage guarantees and makes grow is compatible with the marriage that is not perfect. There might be strained relationship either between husband and wife, or with the children, or failure, times of feeling depressed or guilty. Jesus' presence helps that couple and all couples on the journey to growing in spiritual relationship through love.

ACTION

(i) Let's take seriously the idea that there is a close connection between:
   • God's love for his people
   • Christ's love for us and
   • our love for one another.
   What does this tell us about God, about Jesus and about us?

(ii) Discuss:
   In what ways you as a couple could further welcome Jesus into your marriage?
   Have you experienced provision of wisdom and strength to maintain unity? How?
   Have you experienced Jesus revealing his plans and intentions for you as a couple?
   Have you noticed holiness through Jesus' presence in your marriage?

(iii) Jesus cannot be seen but perhaps it is possible to experience him. How does this happen in our family?

(iv) What are three things we could do in our marriage and/or family that would invite Jesus to be more present?

(v) What are some ways in which Jesus' presence in our marriage becomes real to me?

3. GOD AT WORK THROUGH THE HOLY SPIRIT

- EXPERIENCE

A Spirit-filled Christian Marriage

One person suggested to me, 'It would help if you can describe what a Spirit-filled Christian Marriage looks like'. Another practical-minded person said, 'I hope you will compress your knowledge in one or two working models of family life with do-it-yourself instructions'! I am not sure that anyone can so structure the Holy Spirit. I do know what a Spirit-filled family feels like to enter: there is a sense of life, sharing and loving acceptance. The simplest do-it-yourself recipe I could offer would be: Pray to the Holy Spirit to come and work in your marriage and family, and, as one lady said, 'Go home and do it! Go home and love!'

Understanding the Holy Spirit as the **Love** of God helps us. Love is at the heart of marriage. The Spirit works in Christian Marriage by deepening the Love present. Love makes a Christian Marriage Spirit-filled.

The Holy Spirit does make all the difference. The Spirit goes deeper into the lives of the spouses and their family to let Love touch and heal them. It is the Spirit who will be at hand to help a parent face him/herself when replays of their own upbringing and of the relationship they had with their own parents surface. I think the following experience helps us understand that.

Angela is a beautiful mother and wife, tender, sensitive, good with her hands, whether it be at cooking or doing a bit of home decorating. One night, Angela and Danny were at table. Something quite trivial got under Danny's skin. It brought to a head the tension of the day's work at the shop. His hand crashed on the table: 'Don't contradict. Mark *will* go to the children's party!' 'Oh, my God,' thought Angela, 'he's going to hit me!' Memories of her drunken father beating her mother flooded back. 'Please God, don't let Danny hit me,' she fearfully felt inside. Silence. Angela withdrew into herself. The meal gone sour. Small talk. At dishes time Danny did repent of his outburst of anger and gave Angela a sign of love. That relieved the tension and helped them for that night.

It goes much deeper than Danny and Angela may realise. Danny needs to examine his reactions and how he is dealing with the tension of his work. He may need to recall how his parents sorted issues out and check he is not repeating some of his father's authoritarian style. Parents can slip into repeating their own parents' type of behaviour especially when children arrive. Danny needs to pray for the Spirit to show him if this is happening and what he has to do about it. Angela needs a fuller healing of her relationship with her father. This will come from further understanding of how her father affected her past. She needs God's help to break wrong links with that past. She is unconsciously running the risk of repeating her mother's role; by withdrawing into herself, Angela could elicit a strong, even physical, reaction from Danny to get her to snap out of it.

Angela needs the Spirit to help her forgive her father, even if her feelings are still not positive about him. She needs to invite the healing Love of God into her relationship with her father. She should address any resentment held in her heart against her father. It is her lack of forgiveness of her father that is negatively affecting her present love for herself and for Danny. Danny could profitably ask the Spirit to help him understand why he, as man and father, triggers off Angela's past. With mutual love and prayer and, quite possibly, outside help, Danny and Angela will grow in love and not repeat the past. This is the proper work of the Holy Spirit: to enlighten, to bring repentance, to help forgive, to heal and to increase love.

One couple expressed this healing process beautifully in a prayer they would say:

> Thank you, God, for your bountiful Love.
> You forgive us and keep on forgiving us.
> You pour your Love into us.
> You heal us.
> We forgive anyone in our past who may be negatively affecting our present love for each other and the children: parents, family, friends or others. . .
> Fill us with your Love.
> Heal us by that Love.
> Help us let that Love flow to each other.
> May your Love flow through both of us to our children and to all other people.
> We ask this in Jesus' Name. Amen.

Frances nicely summed up the role of the Spirit in Marriage. 'As I see it, the Spirit works in us so we fully develop the talents and qualities we have been given. Then our married life takes on the special Christian character it should.'

Mind you, the Holy Spirit presents us with a few surprises and a sense of humour to help us through. The Spirit 'blows where it pleases' (Jn 3:8) and can stir up apparently calm waters. There is a long-term reason for this, as God wants to heal deeply and there may need to be a lancing of the boil before true love and relationship can flourish. You will have your own examples. It is a point of encouragement, too. When things seem to be going wrong, God has not abandoned us. Wait, pray, ask guidance. 'We are well aware that God works with those who love him, those who have been called in accordance with his purpose, and turns everything to their good' (Rom 8:28).

Anyway, Miriam told me how, early in their marriage, her husband Ben used to keep the peace, faithfully meeting all the wants she had: the washing was collected; the re-cycling bins emptied; the service was great. Ben uncon-sciously made it worse by reminding Miriam when she was starting to express that something was not quite right: 'What's the matter? I've done everything you wanted me to do'. Finally, Miriam exploded, 'Hey! What I need is a real person who can think and act for himself and relate to me deeply. Someone who can meet my **needs**, not just fulfil all my wants. I don't want to be married to a peace-keeping slave!'

A work of the Spirit? The Holy Spirit certainly helped them both talk and pray it through and meet on a new personal level. So the Spirit can help at surprising times.

The humorous side? One example was when I had naively written to a young couple, commenting too glowingly on the beauty of their two young children, 'You are just like the Spirit-filled marriage of the psalms. You know the one, "Your wife a fruitful vine . . . your children round your table like shoots of an olive tree" ' (Ps 128:3). A rather cryptic reply came back from Aime: 'The fruitful vine, indeed! Children like olive shoots round the table! Humph! And a big mess on the floor!'

I rest my case. Couples, you can really tap into the Love of the Holy Spirit to transform your own relationship, bringing healing to the past, making your marriage Spirit-filled and giving you energy to 'go home and love'.

- SPIRITUAL REFLECTION

The Holy Spirit, inner energy for Christian couples

The Holy Spirit is an inner energy for spouses. The Spirit helps their daily effort to work at relationship and grow in love within Christian Marriage. This inner energy is a two-fold love, the Love of God and that love in the spouses which is necessary for the day to day living of their marriage vows. We have already spoken a lot about God's Love in marriage and how it finds expression in the love of spouses and the community of the family. Here we get in touch with another aspect, the source of that love, the Holy Spirit.

The Holy Spirit is within and without a married couple. The Spirit is the Personal Love of God and so comes from outside a couple. The Holy Spirit is also the inside energy who promotes the love between husband and wife and so finds a home right at the heart of Christian Marriage. I suppose this aspect touches that practical cry from the heart we all make: 'Oh, I wish I had the energy to do this or that. . .' For the Christian that inner energy is the Holy Spirit.

Some of you reading this may be quite familiar with who the Holy Spirit is and be at home with the role the Spirit has in your life. I remind you that there is always more the Spirit can do in you, in your marriage and in your family life. Pray to the Holy Spirit to make you both more open to the inner energy and Love the Spirit provides. Pray to be yet more empowered to make your love like the Love of God and so very fruitful for yourselves and for others.

Some of you may be asking, 'How do I get to know the Holy Spirit more personally? I have been confirmed; how do I release the energy I received then to transform my marriage and make it Spirit-filled? We are trying to live the Gospel values in our marriage and lead a good life; how can we experience more of the Holy Spirit working with us?'

Pray to the Holy Spirit, right now even, and ask for the wisdom and understanding to see what to do. Ask, and keep on asking, for the Holy Spirit to come alive in each of you personally and in both of you as a couple. The Spirit provides the essential Fire of Love for your marriage. Pray that that Fire be kindled in your marriage and that you see God working. Pray to get to know the Spirit as a Personal Friend to you both, energising you and guiding you. All of us may need to look again at the Bookmark provided with this book. It is designed to help precisely in this area.

We can appreciate how the Holy Spirit is the inner energy of Christian Marriage and Family Life by seeing how the Spirit is present in the Trinity. We saw the Community of Love which is the Trinity's. This Life and Love moves outwards and is shared with married couples. God sends the Holy Spirit out with the mission of making men and women one in love and community, in a life like God's. The Holy Spirit is the Love of Father for Son and Son for Father. One of my students once likened the Holy Spirit to the Glue of Love which binds the Life of God! The Spirit is an essential member of the Community of the Trinity. It is only natural that God should work through the Holy Spirit in Christian married love and community.

One of the first ways the Spirit works is to unify Christian partners in their marriage. It is that Glue at work. The Spirit shows each partner the uniqueness and dignity their partner has as a son or daughter of God:

The unity of marriage, distinctly recognised by our Lord, is made clear in the equal personal dignity which must be accorded to man and wife in mutual and unreserved affection (49,2).

This has special value today when there is renewed stress on the equality of husband and wife and the need for marriage to be a partnership. A sound understanding of the equal Life and Love in the Trinity will ensure that deep mutual respect in Christian Marriage, too.

God is a great respecter of persons. God works in marriage to make spouses and children more fully personal in their love and family life. The Spirit completes the work of Jesus Christ by 'restoring, perfecting and elevating' married love. Through the Spirit, spouses find healing by finding their deepest identity.

God's work is then taken up by the spouses who in turn heal each other by forgiveness and love. The couple minister in love to each other. As we have all experienced, there is no healer quite like love. That healing love is the part of the secret of a good marriage.

Healing is so important. There is much in our lives which can scar us and which we will bring into the marriage relationship, too. Healing can be helped very much by the Holy Spirit. The Spirit is healing Love. The Spirit is present in marriage to make the spouses holy and complete persons who practise a firm and generous love.

If you sense you need that healing action of the Holy Spirit in yourself or in your married life, stop now and pray for it. We have provided a prayer in the **ACTION** section below that may help you find the right words.

The fruits of the Holy Spirit
in Christian Marriage

God is at work through the Holy Spirit to complete married love in fruitfulness and community. The Spirit links community and love, enabling men and women's love to be fruitful. Only when they are freed from fear can men and women truly love. 'Perfect love drives out fear' (1 Jn 4:18). That Love is the Holy Spirit. God works through the Spirit so partners can freely love each other and bear fruit in their lives. This is expressed when we say, 'We believe in the Holy Spirit, the Lord, the Giver of Life'. The Holy Spirit is the Spirit of life, of fruitfulness. The fruits of the Holy Spirit's presence are outlined in Paul's letter to the people of Galatia: 'love, joy, peace, patience, kindness, goodness, truthfulness, gentleness and self-control' (Gal 5:22). A Christian couple will ask the Holy Spirit to deepen these qualities in their love.

Linked with this idea of fruitfulness, God works through the Holy Spirit to form community. The Spirit completes the fruitfulness of the couple's love in community. Love and community are related in the Spirit. This relating has a social aspect and a smaller, family aspect.

At the social level, we see the full power of the Spirit animating and drawing all life together in God. The plan of Love and the result of the Spirit of God working in married love is to unite their whole lives in God. The effect of Love is harmony within oneself and with others. I have certainly witnessed this harmony and been privileged to share in the development of it in ordinary families as they have discussed whether to go on holiday or save for a bigger car to serve the family, or in the sadder times of the loss of a dear parent or the miscarriage of a baby. The Spirit comes on all these occasions to help each member of the family personally and socially.

At the family level also, the relation of love to community is effected by God working through the Spirit. The Spirit makes the husband and wife's love fruitful and constructive. The Spirit provides the driving force that ensures the couple and family's love goes out to help form a family spirit of love everywhere.

Through the link of married love and community, the Holy Spirit releases the presence of Christ in marriage and manifests the true nature of God's family. It is in this context we read:

> 'The Christian family ... will show forth to all, Christ's living presence in the world, and the authentic nature of the Church, by the love and generous fruitfulness of the spouses, by their unity and fidelity and by the loving way in which all members of the family co-operate with each other' (48,4).

The character of the Spirit's presence is to effect 'communion of life' in Christ (50,3). The Spirit's presence ensures the life of the marriage. Without the Spirit, Christian Marriage becomes closed in on the two spouses, and the marriage will, to all intent, die. The effect of the Holy Spirit is to keep the partners' love alive and always fruitful.

ACTION

(i) We have seen various ways in which the Holy Spirit
works such as:
  showing each partner the uniqueness and dignity
  their spouse has as a son or daughter of God;
  ensuring that a couple love each other as friends;
  making partners deeper lovers;
Is each of these a reality in our lives?
Are there blocks to the Spirit moving in me/us?
Do we need to cry,
> 'Come, Holy Spirit,
> shine forth your light;
> bring us truth and
> heal us'?

(ii) The following meditation could be used as a response.
Consider praying it as a couple daily.
> Come to us, Holy Spirit,
>   as you came to Mary and the Apostles.
> Open our minds that we may see
>   you at work in our lives.
> Send Love into our hearts
>   like a Flame of Fire.
> Change our lives by the
>   power of your Spirit
> So we can do God's work on earth and
>   bring our children and other people
> with us to heaven.   Amen.

4. GOD AT WORK THROUGH THE FAMILY OF THE CHURCH

- EXPERIENCE

'We're in the Church together'

I remember being at a conference on the Christian Family where we had a keynote song, 'We are the Church'. It had actions that went with the words. The chorus was: 'I am the Church; You are the Church; We are the Church together. All around the world, all who follow Jesus, We're in the Church together'. It was sung with gusto and reinforced the theology that baptised believers in Jesus Christ form a Family called 'Church'.

At the heart of this bigger Family are married couples and their families. There is a twofold movement: God touches marriage and family life through the Family of the Church; God also uses marriage and family to build up the Church Family.

Bob recalled how at one discussion he was surprised when the question was raised, 'How can the family serve the Church?' 'I always felt the only question you can ask is "How can the Church serve the family?" I've learnt they are to serve each other. Marriage and family and the Church are linked. I suppose you could say Christian Marriage is given life by God through the Church, but Marriage in turn gives life to the Church.'

Other couples see the link of Jesus with his Church as the basis for their own sense of the Church Family. Jacinta and Gary see the relationship of Jesus to the Church Family as a partnership. 'Jesus loving his Church and always being

there to help it. Jesus has unselfish love for us. That finally
proved itself when he laid down his life for his Church.
Partnership seems a key word to us in describing Christian
Marriage today. We can see that partnership in the way
Jesus, and the Church people he loves, should interact'.

That partnership is expressed in prayer and communication. Michael and Hannah tell us, 'Just as Jesus prayed for
his Church and taught us how to communicate with his
Father and to love one another, so it's nice to say a prayer
together, just "off the cuff". The closeness you feel after
this is wonderful. We believe a good word for communication is "reveal". In revealing ourselves, we open up and let
each other see inside. We share both strong and weak points.
After some time, we get to the stage where we are one; two
individuals, but one in marriage'. Michael and Hannah have
expressed what I am sure Jesus wants for Christian Marriage
and his Church: unity through prayer and communication
in love.

The relationship of Jesus with his Church needs to come
down to earth and find practical expression by members
of the Church. 'One way the Church can help,' says Sandra,
mother of five, 'is by providing a day-care centre. There
could be a Group who help mothers, taking their children
out for a walk. Mothers who are pregnant, or parents who
just need a break, can have a rest. They could have their
own baby-sitting circle.' I believe this is Christianity in a
form that proves the Church Family is real.

I am sure this is the way God wants us to live. Maybe
not every local Church can have a Day Care Centre, but
every Church must have smaller groupings where people
care for each other. This is what 'Church' is about. Without
this support, worship itself may lack the ring of truth. I

believe marriage and family life is a litmus test for how loving a Church is. Are husbands and wives honoured? Are they supported in bringing up their children? Are family activities a regular part of Church life? I believe this sort of Christianity proves God has been allowed to work. It can make the difference whether people stay in a Church or not, whether their own marriage and family life is happy or not.

I think right now of a family where the mother had to take her child to a hospital in another town for specialised surgery, and stay there for extended periods of time over different months. The local Church people were magnificent in their care for the other children and in supporting her husband providing 'heat-up' food and other help. Since then, that couple has, in their turn, been most generous in helping others. That living example illustrates the point for me. We are the Church together. God works through people to support marriage and family. God works through marriage and family to give practical life and love to the Family of the Church.

This sense of Church and Family often gets inspiring leadership in the lives and dedication of married Christian Ministers and their wives. I personally would not be as enriched a priest as I am without the support some of them have given me. I have in mind two Christian leaders who would meet with me for lunch and prayer every second Wednesday for several years. They and their wives give marvellous witness to God at work in Christian Marriage and Family. I honour them and others like them. They managed to give this witness with that sparkle of fun which is a sign of true Christianity. They discovered I had a weakness for parsley. At one of our Christmas gatherings I was sat down to − you have guessed it − a plate full of parsley!

Another example is my cousin, the late Donald Duncan, a Presbyterian minister. He and his wife put Christianity into practice by adoption of a Chinese girl into their family. Such examples give me evident proof of God at work through them to build up the Church community.

Giuseppina and Raffaele proved the effectiveness of the witness of Christian Marriage and family within the Church Family even among those who are not practising Christian neighbours. They were farmers. Years before they had killed one of their chickens for a sick lady on the next property. Down the years they showed similar kindnesses. They did not see the fruit of all this until the lady was dying. She told Guiseppina as she nursed her, that she had given up any contact with the Church community because of a row over her marriage. 'Now I want you to call a priest. It's the love you and Raffaele, and the children, live out together, and the way you've loved me, that makes me feel part of the Family again.'

• SPIRITUAL REFLECTION

The link of Christian Marriage and Christ's Church

> The well-being of the individual person and of both human and Christian society is closely bound up with the healthy state of conjugal and family life (47,1).

What happens in Christian Marriage affects what happens in Society and in God's Family, the Church.

God is at work through the Church and Jesus Christ in Christian Marriage to establish a loving community or partnership between the couple. Married couples are 'directed and enriched by . . . the salvific action of the Church' (48,2). Christian Marriage finds its direction and nourishment from the saving power that comes to it from the Church family.

The Church is God's family. God loves that family. The Church is the 'assembly of people', chosen by God, who find their centrepoint in Jesus Christ. The Church family enriches Christian Marriage as a smaller family within the Church. Just as we cannot separate Jesus from the Church family, so Christian Marriage and family cannot be cut off from that family. We now examine how God works in Christian Marriage through the Church family.

When we speak about Christian Marriage and the Church, we must not lose sight of the fact that the community of love which is marriage, finds its root source in God's community. God works in a community or family way. God sets up the marriage community in a way that the love and life of a couple and their family echo in a domestic way the Love and Life God wants to share with us. This is a beautiful way to work with us. It is quite a challenge too.

At the heart of this domestic church is the relationship of Jesus Christ with God's Church family. Jesus' union with the Church is presented as being like the relationship of a husband to his spouse. Here is a model union of love for the married couple to imitate, to ponder and draw strength from for their own love and family life.

> The Christian family springs from marriage which is an image and a sharing in the partnership of love between Christ and the Church (48,4).
>
> Christ . . . has blessed [married] love . . . modelled on Christ's own union with the Church (48,2).

The Scriptural reference to Jesus' link with the Church and its parallel with Christian Marriage, is Chapter Five of the Letter to the Ephesians. 'This mystery has great significance, but I am applying it to Christ and the Church' (Eph 5:32; from 5:21-33). The relationship of Jesus Christ and his Church has special meaning for Christian Marriage.

Other couples see the link of Jesus with his Church as the basis for their own sense of the Church family. It is a model of loving union. To build a loving community in Christian Marriage, the partners should base their life on union with Jesus Christ. God's working through the model union of Jesus Christ and the Church community is not an external, static relationship, as though couples looked at some design in a book. God makes it effective within the love and community of the spouses.

Marriage produces the effect is symbolises. The husband receives from God the grace to love his wife generously, deeply, even to be prepared to sacrifice himself for her, just as Jesus loves the Church. So too, the wife receives the grace to love her husband and be faithful to him as the Church loves Jesus Christ.

Each spouse expresses the Love of Jesus Christ to that section of the Church which is their partner. The Love of Jesus Christ for that part of the people of God who is their partner, passes through a spouse's love for his or her partner. Since each is also part of the Church family, the people of God in each receives the expression of the Love of Jesus Christ through the love of their partner for him or her.

That deserves reading again. Maybe even with a prayer to see the beautiful insight that is there. The union of Jesus Christ and his Church fully expresses itself in a couple's partnership as spouses. It is in this way that Christian

Marriage is an image of the union of Jesus Christ with the Church.

Building the family of God

We now take up two points: God builds up Christian Marriage through the members of the Church family; God also builds up the Church family through Christian Marriage.

Firstly, God is at work in Christian Marriage by using different members of the Church. God calls on all Christians

> to promote the values of marriage and the family. [They are to] overcome obstacles and make provision for the requirements and advantages of family life arising at the present day (52,3).

The Christian community is to unite in supporting marriage and family life. This is not setting up a Christian ghetto, but a personal and practical effort to sort out the difficulties and build on the strengths within married life. The Church family is a body of persons who go out into homes to meet and encourage spouses and provide for their needs.

God is at work through Christians in a human way. God stimulates and uses the 'Christian instincts of the faithful, and the right moral conscience of men and women' (52,3). God particularly wants Christians to use the 'witness of their own lives' (52,3) and join with all of good will, be they parents, work mates, teachers or those in public office. Christians of the Church are to support all healthy forces which promote the family. Church people become a living, open group who effectively cooperate with God in helping married life develop.

Secondly, Christian married life is like an extension of the family of God and indeed 'enriches (God's) family from day to day' (50,1). God is at work in the persons in marriage and family life to build up the Church family. This happens when spouses have children, including an 'estimation of the good . . . of the Church' in exercising responsible parenthood' (50,2).

With Jesus Christ's strength, a Christian couple can complete their mission of helping build up the Kingdom of God, which on earth is the Church family. The text sums up what we have been saying:

> '(Christian couples and their children) will show forth to all, Christ's living presence in the world, and the authentic nature of the Church, by (their) love and generous fruitfulness . . . by their unity and fidelity, and by the loving way in which all members of the family co-operate with each other' (48,4).

ACTION

(i) The family is a basic, or domestic Church which is involved in love and service. What are three things we can do as a family to:
   – show our love for each other?
   – demonstrate the Church family in action to those around us?

(ii) How could we as a family offer support, love and friendship to those of our parish who are lonely and 'left out' of activities?

(iii) What have we, as a couple, to offer for building up the wider Church family?

5. GOD AT WORK
   BEYOND THE FAMILY

- EXPERIENCE

'Christian family life is possible today'

'We feel the witness of a basically secure, happy and loving family is one which spreads far and wide,' Matthew and Josie shared with us. 'A family that welcomes each one's friends, that has room for one more, whether it be to stay, for a meal, or to play, is responding to Jesus' call: "For I was hungry and you gave me food, I was thirsty and you gave me drink, I was a stranger and you made me welcome..." (Mt 25:35).

A home doesn't have to be palatial, or even tidy, to be welcoming. It is the attitude that's important. Warm acceptance and a sandwich is worth more in Christian witness than a lavish meal with wine and candles laid on as if you were trying to impress. As parents, we try to let our children know they can always bring their friends home. Our neighbours realise we will lend a hand if we can. We aim to proclaim the Good News in everything we do.'

Other couples found it worked the other way, too. 'We often receive help from neighbours, for example, with baby-sitting. We try to spend leisure time with others who share our values. We can learn a lot from the strengths and weaknesses of the couples around us, from partners we meet at Church, and by taking opportunities to serve others.'

On the other hand, couples were not slow to point out some of the negative pressures on them, things like the temptation to conform to other people's material values, the lack of space at times, for instance in house design, with little privacy or space where children can play or study as they grow up. 'We find it hard to help our children cope with the outside pressures forced on them, too. For ourselves, it is more a question of trying to balance the priorities the children, Church and Community place on it.'

This witness overflows to the work scene. Kerry shared how God was at work through his own workplace: 'God is present by the attitude I show in the way I work and in how I deal with the persons I meet. I can witness to my relationship to my wife Anna when the talk gets around to the topic of marriage or our wives. The same chance to witness exists when God comes into the conversation. God gives me a personal sense of security at work. I am satisfied with what I do and try to help others. I don't feel over-pressured to measure up to their expectations or to depend on what they think of me. I want to reveal the positive effect God has in my marriage, whether the topic comes up directly or I show it indirectly through my behaviour.'

'From time to time, Jocelyn and I have to spend time discerning just what God wants us to be committed to. We have a family relaxation time all of us can do together. We don't set impossible goals. We have to watch our finances and petrol costs, live with tension, feel tired, laugh together. The key for us is letting the Love of God enter our hearts and do our best to show that Love to others around us.'

'My dear Kath,' writes Denis, 'is as busy as a bee! I don't see her for dust at times, but we still find time to just be ourselves, which is an important thing. Kath has an extremely full calendar as far as clinic work with Natural Family Planning is concerned. She has the ability to do the job well. Largely, through her influence, we appear to be attracting more couples from within and outside the

Church. We enjoy that work together and sometimes we are able to show the partners what wonderful work God is doing in their lives.'

'You know, I'm really under great pressure from my work mates because I don't follow many of the ads. We often have just a big jug of water in the fridge in summer, not the advertised fruit juices. I'm constantly questioned, 'How do you manage with your five children?" Many of those who ask are childless after three to five years' marriage. I think we are there to help show them Christian family life is possible today.'

- SPIRITUAL REFLECTION

The salvation of the world

To complete the study of God at work in Christian Marriage, it is important to realise that God's work does not stop within the family unit of parents and children. God's action reaches outside them beyond their marriage and family. Family members themselves are drawn to have union with God in heaven as their final goal. Then God is at work through the family community to influence other families and the wider social community.

God's full working through Christian Marriage is shown when the couple and family reveal God's Love and the nature of the Church family to all people, whether they be neighbours or members of the wider society. The family is to radiate the presence of Jesus Christ and God's Love. Their apostolate as church is to manifest to the world the true nature of family and community. To be truly like the Church, couples need to live in a way that shows God's Love to others.

God works through those men and women of good will who 'esteem marriage' and who form the 'healthy public opinion' which recognises authentic married love (49,3). God will be behind 'everyone who exercises an influence in community and social groups (for) the welfare of marriage and the family' (52,2) and those groups who can affect married persons and the family positively, for example, civil authorties including legislators, the media and scientists (52,2 and 4).

Here is a very important area for ecumenical life. Christians must unite for the growth of marriage and family life and a better society. God is at work through many people and institutions in the wider social community to influence the family community to the good. The Christian family seeks to build on what is good in society and the world. We are not living an ideal cut off from other men and women. We will often discover God in the good people around us. 'Christians cannot regard marriage and family as a purely private affair.' God has established and stabilised marriage for the good of society (48,1). Because of this, Christian couples should be conscious of their solidarity with all men and women.

God sees no clash between generations, but uses the different ages to spread wisdom, tolerance and harmony. A lack of God's presence will bring lack of harmony. In God's plan there is no clash between the family and society: a sound family life, a sound social life; a strong Christian home, a strong Christian community.

God achieves this harmony through parents and children. The family unit must take part in 'a much needed cultural, psychological and social renewal in matters of marriage and family' (49,3). That sounds rather ideal. It comes down to things like welcoming the children's friends home, inviting a solo parent or pensioner to a meal or for a visit, helping migrants settle, being an active part of the Neighbourhood Support Group, and possibly helping with a needy child. The Christian can also do so much to counter the niggly quarrels we can meet in the office or work-place, the concern for social promotion, gaining more money and the restless quest for success. If Christians share together and support one another, God can really work more clearly through them. We have a mission to be God's Love at work in our world.

This needs reflecting on. We need to work through the real tension between keeping the relationship of husband and wife strong, and being open to serve others in community. If we do build up sound Christian marriages, those couples will have the resources to go out to the wider community. At times they will work directly with those in need. At other times, they will concentrate on strengthening their relationship in Jesus Christ and fostering the Christian upbringing of their family. In view of the interrelation between family and society, it is impossible to accept being a Christian family without taking part in pastoral work and in social and cultural action.

Members of the Christian family must be truly good Christians to achieve the full working of God in society. Christians will turn to God who works to support and love them so that they can achieve their mission in building up society. In this way, Christian married couples and their families will work for a just society. They will fulfil their Christian vocation in Jesus to bring God's Love and Life into the world. What is in question all along is the salvation of the world.

ACTION

(i) Given that God is at work within our marriage, what are some steps we could take to bring God's power and Love to those outside it?

(ii) 'Christians cannot regard marriage and family as a purely private affair' (50,2). Are there ways in which our marriage affects others? How could we make more room for God to use our family for others?

(iii) What are the most significant bad influences that society has on our family? What are some practical steps we could take to overcome them?

(iv) Discuss some ways in which we, as a family, can ensure a healthy balance between time spent within the family and time spent outside the family.

CONCLUSION

God is vitally concerned about your marriage. God will make your marriage work. God has invested in you, in your relationship and in your children. God will not let that investment slip away in vain. Motivated by concern and Love, God guarantees working to help sustain you and your family.

One of the key teachings of Christian Spiritual Theology is that the initiative in spiritual life and growth is God's. We receive. We are chosen. We are loved first. The First Letter of John captures that idea: 'God is Love . . . it is not we who loved God, but God loved us . . . let us love, then, because God first loved us' (1 Jn 4:8,10,19).

A great load is lifted from us. This book has not been about mechanical techniques to make marriage work. It has provided a lot of experiences to show God working. It aims to take away that desire bred into most of us, 'I have to work harder at this; if only I try to use this and this, things will work out'. *God at Work* wants to change us from task-centred people to trusting, heart-centred people, from people who have to **do** everything ourselves, who try to earn God's Love and our partner's approval by busily achieving it all ourselves. Can you sense God saying to you now, 'Let **Me**

do it. Don't depend on yourself; depend on me and my Love
for you and yours'? What a relief! What a refreshing life-
giving breeze, like standing on the beach at the beginning
of a holiday breathing in the sea air. Even when we are not
consciously aware of God's presence or even slipping back
into doing things by our own effort, God is loving, waiting,
guiding, embracing, encouraging, hoping to get a chance
to show what can be done in Christian Marriage.

So we need to get rid of the blocks that prevent God
working as fruitfully as is possible in our marriage. We need
to trust God and actively ask God to work in our marriage.
The emphasis of this book has been on God's work. The
question to ask yourself is 'Will I cooperate with God's
action?' Do not try to do it all; invite God in to work at
it with you. Ask the Holy Spirit to bring your marriage
relationship to life, to become even more loving.

> 'Holy Spirit, help me/us see how God can work in this
> or that area of our marriage, in us personally and in our
> children. Transform our marriage. Help our children; help
> us open ourselves even more to your action. Prevent us
> doing it all so you have no room to work. Come and work
> with us. Show us how God is at work in our marriage.'

This may help those Christian spouses who are the sole
active Christian in a marriage. God has an investment in
your marriage, too. God wants to heal your relationship from
its roots. God is doing things in your marriage through you.
Do not try to do it all yourself. Do not try so hard to win
your partner over, to please him or her, to make him or
her a Christian. Take heart. Let God work away at your
love and family life more. Spend a little time with God to
let God's Love touch you and refresh you in your deepest
self. Go back to your marriage and family refreshed and
conscious of God doing the work.

A couple does not require a great deal of effort to let God work in their lives. They just have to be couples and parents who have invited God to share in their lives. Once that invitation is placed, God can work, even when they are not consciously thinking about God's presence. I hope no one who has read this book puts it down with the thought: 'That's beyond me; I/we could never measure up to that standard!'. If any feel that way, think again. The point is that **God** will do the work. God does the measuring up, not us. Nothing is beyond God. All God asks is to get a foot in on the inside of your relationship and married life. God is not out to produce extraordinary couples who are super-holy or super-organised. God wants to let Love and Graciousness work in the ordinary events that make up Christian Marriage.

To test this, think again about the numerous experiences we have shared with you. They are all from real people: real lives; real couples; real marriages; real families. Sure, you and I may have all sorts of feelings and reactions to them or to other points raised in the book. We may feel it is too difficult or that these experiences are not for us. If we can only let God in to encourage and enlighten us, God will work in **our** ordinary experiences, too. Invite God to do that. Let it begin with us!

For those of you who like diagrams and can sum things up in a picture, the following may help. For those for whom diagrams are confusing, please bear with us for a moment.

GOD AT WORK IN CHRISTIAN MARRIAGE

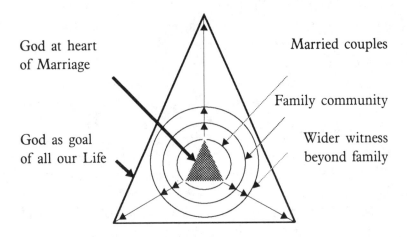

God at heart
of Marriage

Married couples

Family community

God as goal
of all our Life

Wider witness
beyond family

(the arrows indicate the energy flow of God's Love and Life)

God is the beginning and end of our lives. The two triangles represent God at the centre or heart of a couple's life and God at the outside, as the goal embracing them and everything else. The first, inner circle is the Christian couple themselves. God provides the unifying point of Christian Marriage, working as the wellspring and source of all their love and community life.

The dynamic force of God's Love urges the couple to spread their love to others, first of all to their own family (the second circle) and then expanding further out to touch other people, people God will arrange for the couple and family to meet throughout their lives (the third circle). This last circle will include the family of the Church and the culture, work and daily lives of many others as well, so they too can grow in knowledge of God's Love and Life.

God's working in Christian Marriage has a scope far beyond what we might first think. God wants to work through marriage and family life to build up a community family of all men and women. The outer triangle speaks of God's Kingdom which is begun on earth and will be fully realised in heaven.

In the Introduction I spoke of being on a journey. This book is a step on our journey. Maybe now we will journey with less pressure on ourselves and greater trust in God doing the work. Marriage is a beginning. As a straightforward farming friend said when he heard I was writing a book. 'The only comment I would make is Marriage is the first stage of learning to really love each other'. How true. God wants to be a key factor in that learning. God has much to teach us.

Part of the learning on that journey will come from children and family life. Something of God working through children is captured by a Maori couple, Rose and Mark, who had three-year old twins,

> I think Awhi and Piri have brought us all so very close in many different ways. I thank God with all my heart that through my children I am finding God's Love more and more. There's so much to learn about God's Love and Understanding. There is so much God wants for everyone and so much we could have to hold near to our hearts. . .

So be encouraged as you take up your journey. You may want to share with some other people or get something going in your parish or area, such as a sharing group to help one another. The book, or some sections of it, may provide reflection and action for you.

Take heart from that promise in the Word of God: 'I am quite confident that the One who began a good work in you will go on completing it until the Day of Jesus Christ comes' (Phil 1:6). God has not placed an investment in you for nothing. God is not at work in your marriage in vain. Above all, pray. Pray for each other. Pray for your family. Pray for others who read this book. Ask the Holy Spirit where your journey leads to now. Ask how you can continue to let God work in your Christian Marriage and family today.

EPILOGUE

At the last gathering I had with the couples who helped me finalise this book, I gained new depth of insight into its title, *God at Work*. Our meeting took place in front of a log fire and we began by spending about fifteen minutes in silent prayer before its warmth and flickering light.

When we shared, what was strongly felt, was God **is** at work in Christian Marriage. The whole theme of the book is to **let** God work. We are to get out of the way so God can love us as couples and family and make Christian Marriage work. It was like the fire we were looking at. The wood was being consumed by the flames. All it had to do was **be** there! The fire does the work, transforming the wood into light and heat. So **God** does the work, transforming Christian Marriage into a life-giving relationship of love and community. As the wood allows itself to be changed, so the task of Christian partners is to allow God to transform the ordinary lives they lead.

Another insight that sharpened as we sat around the fire, sharing among ourselves, was **how** God is at work. God is at work in Christian Marriage in the **ordinary** events that make up a couple's and a family's daily life. God works in the ordinary signs of love a couple shows one another and

their children; in forgiveness and sexuality, in parenting and
the education of children; in the affection and daily fidelity
of partners; in the decisions about when to have prayer
together and how involved to be beyond the family. God
is at work in all these ordinary activities of practical daily
living. The divine enters the human and transforms it with
Love. The ordinariness of marriage is taken up into the
powerful loving force of God and takes on a much deeper
meaning.

This emphasis on God doing the work is captured by
reflecting on how electricity works. This example is written
about by Kay:

> The essential thing about Christian Marriage is the link
> of partners in Jesus Christ. This is a true, dynamic force,
> as real as electricity. We must get this idea across by living
> it, so people will believe it, and God's strength will really
> show. When we press an electric switch we have no doubt
> the current will flow and there will be light and heat and
> we'll see everything better and clearer and be able to cook
> and do all sorts of things. If we really believe there's a force,
> God's Love, at work in Christian Marriage, which is
> generated in the love and community of husband and wife,
> then we won't stop that power flowing.

You know, even as I shared this with the couples, I missed
the point. My emphasis was on how important it was to
turn the switch on. I had slipped back into thinking it all
depended on me and my earning of God's Love by fulfilling
the tasks I had to do. As the couples quickly reminded me,
Kay was emphasising God's work and our getting out of
the way so God's Love could flow. Our role is to believe
and **let** the power of God's Love and strength and Life flow
into ourselves, our marriage, our family.

Of course, the more we let that Love flow, the greater work God can do; the more open we are, the greater the fruitfulness and transformation of our marriage and family life. The more we are disposed to let God work, the more God's Love and Life will be evident, like more electric lights in the home tapping into the electricity flow. That openness is itself a gift. Letting God work is a gift. We need to pray to be able to let God work – that is turning on the switch.

I must admit I was pleasantly surprised myself. It was an exciting, fresh look at something well known, catching a different insight into a familiar scene. As the author, I felt God had been doing a work with me, too, using this book even more powerfully than I realised. God was to transform into very practical terms the theory I was writing to help those who read it. I actually felt: 'Hmm, I'd like to read that book. There's something important to learn there.' The couples chuckled at this!